RAPTURE

AND

RESURRECTION

N.W. Hutchings

All scripture references are from the King James Version unless otherwise stated.

RAPTURE AND RESURRECTION
Copyright © 1992 by Noah W. Hutchings

Printed in the United States of America

Table of Contents

Introduction

The patriarch Job looked beyond his earthly circumstances—a time of pain, suffering, sorrow, and disappointment—to consider a possible reason for his temporal existence, and he cast the question toward the heavens: *"If a man die, shall he live again? . . ."* (Job 14:14).

The life experience of Job is a type of the history of mankind with ups and downs, peace and war, plenty and poverty, happiness and despair, health and pestilence. If this three score and ten of human expectancy is all we have to hope for, then as the agnostic existentialists aver, we are locked in a circle of vacuum with no way to go but inward. If this is all there is to it, then as the apostle declared in his letter to the congregation of Christians at Corinth, *". . . we are of all men most miserable"* (1 Cor. 15:19).

But men like Job and Paul, who had a personal experience with God, received the assurance that their present lives were just the beginning, not the end. Job victoriously answered his own question, *". . . I wait, till my change come. Thou shalt call, and I will answer thee . . ."* (Job 14:14-15).

As we begin this study on resurrection, it is important to clarify our definitions at the beginning. What do we mean by Rapture, and what do we mean by church?

Rapture

The word "rapture" is not found in the King James

Version of the Bible. It is taken from the Latin word *rapere* found in 1 Thessalonians 4:16-17. It means to be caught up, or caught away. Rapture also implies to be caught up in a state of happiness or ecstasy. The word is often used to describe the happiness of a bride on her wedding day. In the Scriptures, Jesus Christ is referred to as the Bridegroom, and the church as His espoused; and the Bible teaches that one day Christ will return and catch up, or rapture His bride. By inserting "rapture" for "caught up" in 1 Thessalonians 4:16-17, we read:

"For the Lord himself shall. descend from heaven with a shout, with the voice of the archangel, and with the trump of God: and the dead in Christ shall rise first: Then we which are alive and remain shall be 'raptured' together with them in the clouds, to meet the Lord in the air: and so shall we ever be with the Lord."

At the return of Jesus Christ, the body of believers who will be translated from this earth to meet the Lord in the air will be divided into two groups—those who have died in Christ, and whose bodies are asleep, and those who will be alive when this great event takes place.

Church

When we say "the church," to whom or what do we refer? In the original Greek, the word *kuriake* meant a building, or a house of God. However, when we speak of the church as a spiritual body, we are not referring to a church building or a collection of church buildings. The Greek word *ecclesia* meant the inclusive members of an organization, and it is used in the New Testament to mean the members of the church as a whole, the members of a local church assembly, or the members or participants of any religious group. A Hindu assembly can be called a church. The Israelites, as a separated body in the wilderness, were called a church (Acts 7:38). Therefore, when we refer to the church, we need to qualify our reference.

Our first qualification is found in Ephesians 3:1-10:

> *"For this cause I Paul, the prisoner of Jesus Christ for you Gentiles, If ye have heard of the dispensation of the grace of God which is given me to you-ward: How that by revelation he made known unto me the mystery . . . Which in other ages was not made known unto the sons of men, as it is now revealed unto his holy apostles and prophets by the Spirit; That the Gentiles should be fellowheirs, and of the same body, and partakers of his promise in Christ by the gospel: Whereof I was made a minister, according to the gift of the grace of God given unto me by the effectual working of his power . . . And to make all men see what is the fellowship of the mystery, which from the beginning of the world hath been hid in God, who created all things by Jesus Christ: To the intent that now unto the principalities and powers in heavenly places might be known by the church the manifold wisdom of God."*

The church to which Paul referred was not the all-Jewish church of the Old Testament, or a Buddhist church, or a Moslem church, or any other group of people living in the past, present, or future. It was a group of people from all races who would believe and be saved by the gospel of Jesus Christ, the power of God unto salvation, during the dispensation of grace. This body, or church, would inherit heavenly places with Christ. It is to this intent and purpose that this church will be caught up to meet the Lord in the air. Those members of this church who have died in the faith of Jesus Christ will be resurrected in immortal bodies. Those who are alive at the coming of the Lord for His church will experience a physical change.

Paul wrote again of this glorious event in 1 Corinthians 15:51-52:

> *"Behold, I shew you a mystery; We shall not all sleep, but we shall all be changed, In a moment, in the twinkling of an eye, at the last trump: for the trumpet shall sound, and the dead shall be raised incorruptible, and we shall be changed."*

Modern science has proven that our earthly bodies of flesh and blood cannot live in outer space for any great length of time, without life support systems. Therefore, at the translation of the church from earth to heavenly places, a physical change will take place. The members of the church of the dispensation of grace, in an inclusive sense, are called the body of Christ, a designation given no other group of believers.

The message to be proclaimed by ambassadors for Christ during the dispensation of grace is unique; the Christian walk before the world is unique; Christian rewards are unique; and their destination and resurrection are unique. The Scriptures state emphatically that the dispensation of grace, also known as the church age, will end at a definite period of time. When the age of the church of the dispensation of grace ends, God will call the members of the church out of the world, and only the ones belonging to this particular body of Christ will be partakers in this unique resurrection and translation.

Chapter One

Resurrection Before the Flood

It is not difficult for Christians to accept the promise of resurrection unto eternal life. Paul stated in 1 Corinthians 15, if there is no hope of a life hereafter for those who believe, what does it profit us? We might as well eat, drink, and be merry with the unregenerate masses, for tomorrow we die, and that is the end of life. So the difficulty in teaching about the Rapture of the church is not resurrection or translation, but rather that the resurrection and translation of Christians in this dispensation will be a separate and distinct event in God's program of redemption and resurrection. Therefore, we must place the Rapture of the church in its proper setting within God's complete program for the ages; else, those Christians who are not grounded in dispensational truths will become lost and confused.

The apostle wrote in 2 Peter 3:9 that the Lord is *". . . not willing that any should perish, but that all should come to repentance."* God made Adam with the promise of eternal life (Gen. 3:22). All Adam had to do to live forever was to obey God and eat of the tree of life. It was God's will that Adam eat of the tree of life. But after Adam sinned, he began to die, as God said he would. His flesh began to age, his body became subject to pain and disease, and he began to think evil thoughts against God.

Therefore, the first man was barred from the Garden of Eden and the tree of life. The body of Adam had to die because of sin, just as all born of the flesh of Adam must die. But in God's act of clothing Adam and Eve with the skin of a slain animal, the Creator held out the hope for a future resurrection. We read in 1 Corinthians 15:21-22:

"For since by man came death, by man came also the resurrection of the dead. For as in Adam all die, even so in Christ shall all be made alive."

If the hope of resurrection did not extend from Adam, then God would have had no purpose in allowing the first man and woman to live and bear children. But in order to keep their sinful natures under control, and to keep them from trying to exalt themselves above the Lord as Satan had done, God said in Genesis 3:16-19:

"Unto the woman he said, I will greatly multiply thy sorrow and thy conception; in sorrow thou shalt bring forth children; and thy desire shall be to thy husband, and he shall rule over thee. And unto Adam he said, Because thou hast hearkened unto the voice of thy wife, and hast eaten of the tree, of which I commanded thee, saying, Thou shalt not eat of it: cursed is the ground for thy sake; in sorrow shalt thou eat of it all the days of thy life; Thorns also and thistles shall it bring forth to thee; and thou shalt eat the herb of the field; In the sweat of thy face shalt thou eat bread, till thou return unto the ground; for out of it wast thou taken: for dust thou art, and unto dust shalt thou return."

Ever since God spoke these words, the more affluent the status of man becomes, the more he depends upon his own knowledge and strength, and the less he looks to God in repentance for salvation. But then, God brings man down to the ground again where he can turn his face heavenward for deliverance. As God explained, the burdens and trials of mankind are for man's own good. Without them, no man would ever look to God for salvation and a future life beyond the death of the body. From Adam and Eve came death, but also from Adam and Eve came the hope of resurrection. This promise was given to the first man and the first woman in Genesis 3:14-15:

"And the Lord God said unto the serpent, Because thou hast done this, thou art cursed above all cattle, and above every beast of the field; upon thy belly shalt thou go, and dust shalt thou eat all the days of thy life: And I will put enmity between thee and the woman, and between thy seed and her seed; it shall bruise thy head, and thou shalt bruise his heel."

The bruising of the seed of woman came when Jesus Christ was wounded for our transgressions on the cross to become the firstfruits of resurrection life. And so God's promise of resurrection extends all the way back to Adam.

We read in Genesis, chapters four and five, that Adam and Eve had many sons and daughters, and in the course of time two great men of faith appeared on the earth: Enoch and Noah. We read in Genesis 5:24, *"And Enoch walked with God: and he was not; for God took him."* We read also in Genesis 6:8-9:

"But Noah found grace in the eyes of the Lord . . . Noah was a just man and perfect in his generations, and Noah walked with God."

Of Enoch we read again in Hebrews 11:5-6:

"By faith Enoch was translated that he should not see death; and was not found, because God had translated him: for before his translation he had this testimony, that he pleased God. But without faith it is impossible to please him. . . ."

Of Noah we read in Hebrews 11:7:

"By faith Noah, being warned of God of things not seen as yet, moved with fear, prepared an ark to the saving of his house; by the which he condemned the world, and became heir of the righteousness which is by faith."

The standing of Enoch and Noah before God was the same: grace through faith. Both men pleased God and both men walked with God. One man was translated that he should not see death; the other man was instructed to labor and build an ark to save his household from the flood. Why the difference?

In Enoch, God gave mankind, for all history, a practical example of translation of the body from mortality to immortality. The soul and spirit are already eternal. It is the body that must be changed. Enoch was taken up into heaven; he could not be found on earth. And before he was taken up, he prophesied that God would translate a great host of saints at some future time. We read in Jude 14:

"And Enoch also, the seventh from Adam, prophesied of these, saying, Behold, the Lord cometh with ten thousands of his saints."

Enoch's body was changed in a moment, and he was translated to live for eternity in heaven. Enoch was a type of the church of the dispensation of grace. And like the world searched for Enoch, one day those left behind will be searching for the Christians, but they will all be gone—translated at the Rapture.

But what about Noah? Why was he not translated? We know that two great judgments are determined upon the earth because of the exceeding wickedness of man: the flood and the Great Tribulation. The flood is compared to the Great Tribulation. Jesus said that as it was in the days of Noah, so it would be when He came again. Enoch was translated over the judgment of flood, but Noah and his household had to go through it in the ark. In this, Noah became a type of Israel. The church will be translated over the Great Tribulation, but Israel will go through it, and we read in Zechariah 13:8-9, Romans 11:26, and many other scriptures, that a faithful remnant will be saved.

The ark can be symbolized to mean the salvation of the Jew and Gentile alike in Christ, but in considering the two men from the standpoint of resurrection, Enoch is a type of the church, whose inheritance is in heaven, and Noah is a type of Israel, whose inheritance is on earth. Enoch represents a resurrection of a body of God's people for heavenly places; and Noah represents a resurrection of the saints of Israel for an earthly inheritance. No devout and religious Jew acknowledges any heavenly reward in resurrection, because such a promise is not made to the Old Testament saints. All resurrection to Israel relates to immortality in the Kingdom age, which points forward to a New Heaven and a New Earth. In type we see the translation of the church of the dispensation of grace set apart as a separate event on God's calendar of resurrection, even before the flood.

From the beginning of man's transgression against God, the wages of sin was death, but the gift of God was eternal life through grace, even to those who lived before the flood. Of those antediluvians who were redeemed from Hell and death we read in Hebrews 11:4-6:

"By faith Abel offered unto God a more excellent sacrifice than Cain, by which he obtained witness that he was righteous, God testifying of his gifts: and by it he being dead yet speaketh. By faith Enoch was translated that he should not see death; and was not found, because God had translated him: for before his translation he had this testimony, that he pleased God. But without faith it is impossible to please him: for he that cometh to God must believe that he is, and that he is a rewarder of them that diligently seek him."

Chapter Two

Resurrection From Abraham to David

In our second study on Rapture and resurrection, we will continue from the Old Testament position. In our first chapter, we traced the promise of resurrection from Adam to Enoch and Noah, Enoch a type of the Rapture of the church, and Noah a type of the resurrection of the saints of Israel.

From Noah we go to Abraham, and we read of the patriarch in Hebrews 11:8-10:

> *"By faith Abraham, when he was called to go out into a place which he should after receive for an inheritance, obeyed; and he went out, not knowing whither he went. By faith he sojourned in the land of promise, as in a strange country, dwelling in tabernacles with Isaac and Jacob, the heirs with him of the same promise: For he looked for a city which hath foundations, whose builder and maker is God."*

The only city mentioned in the Bible whose builder and maker is God is the new Jerusalem, and we read again of Abraham in Romans 4:20-21:

"He staggered not at the promise of God through unbelief; but was strong in faith, giving glory to God; And being fully persuaded that, what he had promised, he was able also to perform."

The Scriptures indicate that Abraham's faith in the city of resurrection that God promised him was so strong, that he looked for it wherever he went. When the patriarch visited the Pharaoh in his palace at the capital city of Egypt, he must have seen the Great Pyramid, which many Bible scholars have referred to as a type of the new Jerusalem. When it was originally constructed, the Great Pyramid was overlaid with one hundred forty-four thousand polished limestone blocks, sealed with mortar. Seeing the Great Pyramid may have been one of the factors that led Abraham across the burning Sinai Desert to Egypt. Clarence Larkin wrote:

*"The Great Pyramid is the only form of building that conforms to the symbolic description of the **spiritual building** spoken of in Scripture, of which Christ is said to be the **chief cornerstone**. Ephesians 2:20-22, 'Ye are built upon the foundation of the apostles and prophets, Jesus Christ himself being the chief corner stone; in whom all the building fitly framed together groweth unto an holy temple in the Lord; In whom ye also are builded together for the habitation of God through the Spirit.' There is no **chief cornerstone** in architectural construction but in a building of pyramidal form, and in shape it is exactly like the building that tops out. . . . Being five-sided, there is no place for it in the building until the*

finishing touch is given, and therefore the builders rejected it until needed. So we read of Christ— 'The stone, which the builders disallowed . . . the same is made the head of the corner, and a stone of stumbling and a rock of offence!' The capstone of a pyramid until needed would be in the way, and a 'Stone of Stumbling' and 'Rock of Offence' to the workermen. So with Christ, Paul says—'We preach Christ crucified unto the Jews a stumbling block, and unto the Greeks foolishness,' or, 'Rock of Offence' (1 Cor. 1:23). The capstone of a pyramid is five-sided and five-pointed, with sharp points always sticking up. Anyone falling on it would be 'broken' or injured, and when on its way to its lofty position, were it to fall on anyone, it would 'grind him to powder.' From what has been said we see the Great Pyramid is symbolic of the spiritual building of which Christ is the 'Chief Capstone.' . . . The Great Pyramid, as originally constructed, was built of granite overlaid with white limestone, and its exterior surface was smooth and unmountable, and it appeared like a building let down from Heaven."

It is evident from Scripture that God promised Abraham a mansion in the new Jerusalem. And Abraham believed that what God had promised him, He was able to perform. The city did not come down from Heaven in the life of Abraham, but it is coming in due time according to God's eternal plan and purpose. We read in Revelation 21:2:

"And I John saw the holy city, new Jerusalem,

*coming down from God out of heaven, prepared
as a bride adorned for her husband."*

Abraham will see this great city whose builder and
maker is God. Abraham had the promise of resurrection,
and what God promises, He is able to fulfill. So strong
was the faith of Abraham in resurrection that he was
willing to kill his own son at God's instructions, believing
that God would raise Isaac up again. We read of
Abraham again in Hebrews 11:17-19:

*"By faith Abraham, when he was tried, offered
up Isaac: and he that had received the promises
offered up his only begotten son. Of whom it
was said, That in Isaac shall thy seed be called:
Accounting that God was able to raise him up,
even from the dead. . . ."*

Perhaps none of the heroes of faith had a more
personal assurance from God of resurrection than
Abraham. When Abraham buried Sarah, he mourned
because of their temporary separation, and he paid four
thousand shekels for a suitable burying place for her body
(Gen. 23). He believed God would raise her body from the
dead. The Christian funeral is itself a manifestation of
faith in resurrection. It dates back to the burial of Sarah
by the father of faith, Abraham.

It would be difficult to discuss the hope of resurrection
held by all the Old Testament saints, so from Abraham we
go to Joseph. We read of Joseph in Hebrews 11:22:

*"By faith Joseph, when he died, made mention
of the departing of the children of Israel; and
gave commandment concerning his bones."*

When Joseph died, he was embalmed according to the instructions of the patriarch. The Egyptians originated the science of embalming the body and preparing it for mummification. Joseph also commanded the physicians to embalm the body of Jacob, his father. And we read in Genesis 50:24-26 that when Joseph died, they placed his embalmed body in a coffin. When the children of Israel departed from the land of Egypt, they were to carry his coffin back to the Promised Land, so that when the resurrection of Israel occurred, Joseph would already be in the Kingdom.

From Joseph we go to Moses, one of the most stalwart of the Old Testament saints. His importance to God is seen in the fact that the name of Moses is mentioned more times in the Bible than the name of any other man. We read of Moses in Jude 9:

"Yet Michael the archangel, when contending with the devil he disputed about the body of Moses. . . ."

Why would the Devil dispute with Michael over the body of Moses? Because Michael is the guardian angel of Israel's resurrection. We read in Daniel 12:1-2 that after Michael stands up for God's earthly people Israel during the Tribulation, and he leads the armies of Heaven to a great and final victory over Satan and his angels (Rev. 12:7-10), the resurrection of the saints of Israel, who sleep in the dust of the earth, will occur. We read the scripture in Daniel 12:1-2:

"And at that time shall Michael stand up, the great prince which standeth for the children of thy people: and there shall be a time of trouble,

*such as never was since there was a nation even
to that same time: and at that time thy people*
[meaning Daniel's people Israel] *shall be
delivered, every one that shall be found written
in the book. And many of them that sleep in the
dust of the earth shall awake, some to everlasting
life, and some to shame and everlasting
contempt."*

The only logical explanation for Satan disputing
with Michael over the body of Moses was that Satan did
not want Moses to be resurrected. Scriptural evidence
indicates that Moses will be one of the two supernatural
witnesses of God who will oppose the Antichrist during
three and a half years of the Tribulation, and the
Antichrist will be Satan incarnate. It is no wonder,
therefore, why Satan disputed with Michael over the
body of Moses. So we see from Scripture that even the
Devil believes in resurrection.

From Moses we go to the patriarch Job. The book of
Job was the first book of our Bible to be written. It was
written even before Moses wrote the first five books. Job
is commended in Scripture for his patience in faith, even
under the most extreme suffering and adversity. The hope
of this patriarch was a glorified body. We read these
words of Job in chapter 14:14-15:

*"If a man die, shall he live again? all the days of
my appointed time will I wait, till my change
come. Thou shalt call, and I will answer
thee. . . ."*

Job believed that his body, that was subject to
disease and suffering, would be changed. Job realized that

his body was weak because of sin, but he was strong in faith that God would send a Redeemer to pay the penalty for his sins. We read again in Job 19:25-27:

> *"For I know that my redeemer liveth, and that he shall stand at the latter day upon the earth: And though after my skin worms destroy this body, yet in my flesh shall I see God: Whom I shall see for myself, and mine eyes shall behold, and not another; though my reins be consumed within me."*

God revealed to Job that his Redeemer would come to redeem from sin all who would receive Him as Savior and Lord. Job also said that his Redeemer would stand upon this earth in the latter day, and though his own body would rot away, he would be raised in new flesh to behold his Savior's face.

The Lord Jesus Christ came the first time to die, not only for the sins of Job, but for all who would believe on His Name. He was raised from the dead the third day, and ascended back to God, His Father. He is coming in the latter day, not to die again, but rather to stand upon the earth. Stand, when used both literally and symbolically in the same scripture, means to claim, or take possession. We read of the Lord's return in Zechariah 14:4:

> *"And his feet shall **stand in that day** upon the mount of Olives, which is before Jerusalem . . ."*

We read also of the return of Jesus Christ to this earth in Revelation 10:2-3:

> *". . . he set his right foot upon the sea, and his*

*left foot on the earth, And cried with a loud
voice, as when a lion roareth. . . ."*

Job not only expressed complete faith in the resurrection of his body; he pinpointed the time when his body of
flesh would rise up out of the dust of the earth. He said his
resurrection would come when the Redeemer came to
take possession of the world. And we shall see as we
continue in this study, that all resurrection of the saved is
associated with the second coming of Jesus Christ.

From the patriarch Job we go to King David. Faith
in life everlasting and resurrection from the dead per-
meated the very life and thought of David. His strong
faith in eternal life was manifested at the death of his son
by Bathsheba. We read in 2 Samuel 12:22-23:

*"And he said, While the child was yet alive, I
fasted and wept: for I said, Who can tell whether
God will be gracious to me, that the child may
live? But now he is dead, wherefore should I
fast? can I bring him back again? I shall go to
him, but he shall not return to me."*

The certainty of life beyond the grave was also
beautifully expressed by David in Psalm 23:4-6:

*"Yea, though I walk through the valley of the
shadow of death, I will fear no evil: for thou art
with me; thy rod and thy staff they comfort me.
Thou preparest a table before me in the presence
of mine enemies: thou anointest my head with
oil; my cup runneth over. Surely goodness and
mercy shall follow me all the days of my life: and
I will dwell in the house of the Lord for ever."*

This hope of David is to be understood literally. When Christ returns He will reign as King of kings, but the promise of David in resurrection was that he would be a prince of Israel in the house of the Lord. Of the refounding of Israel in the last days and the return of the Lord, we read in Ezekiel 34:23-24:

> *"And I will set up one shepherd over them, and he shall feed them, even my servant David; he shall feed them, and he shall be their shepherd. And I the Lord will be their God, and my servant David a prince among them; I the Lord have spoken it."*

We read again in Ezekiel 37:25,27:

> *"And they shall dwell in the land that I have given unto Jacob my servant, wherein your fathers have dwelt; and they shall dwell therein, even they, and their children, and their children's children for ever: and my servant David shall be their prince for ever . . . My tabernacle also shall be with them: yea, I will be their God, and they shall be my people."*

The promise of God that the Kingdom will be brought in, the Temple rebuilt, and Jesus reign as King of kings and David as the prince of Israel in the house of the Lord, is referred to as the restoration of the tabernacle of David. We read in Acts 15:15-16:

> *"And to this agree the words of the prophets; as it is written, After this I will return, and will build again the tabernacle of David, which is*

fallen down; and I will build again the ruins thereof, and I will set it up."

Once again we see that the resurrection of saints in the Old Testament is anchored in the glorious return of Jesus Christ. Each saint in the Old Testament was promised his own particular reward, and we read in Hebrews 11:16 that God has prepared for them a city. All resurrection is held in God's power by the authority of Jesus Christ. All the faith of the Old Testament saints in resurrection through the coming Redeemer was reflected in the words of Jesus recorded in John 11:25-26:

". . . I am the resurrection, and the life: he that believeth in me, though he were dead, yet shall he live: And whosoever liveth and believeth in me shall never die. . . ."

Chapter One

Resurrection of Israel

Resurrection in the books of the prophets has mainly to do with the future resurrection of Israel, because the main subject of the prophets is God's Kingdom promises to His earthly people.

The children of Israel who believed God and kept His commandments were partakers of the promise of a literal kingdom here on earth. Although the thirty-seventh chapter of Ezekiel is usually interpreted as a symbolic prophecy concerning the spiritual rebirth of Israel in the last days, and their regathering back into the land, it should also be understood literally as referring to the resurrection of the saints. We read in Ezekiel 37:11-13:

"Then he said unto me, Son of man, these bones are the whole house of Israel: behold, they say, Our bones are dried, and our hope is lost: we are cut off for our parts. Therefore prophesy and say unto them, Thus saith the Lord God; Behold, O my people, I will open your graves, and cause you to come up out of your graves, and bring you into the land of Israel. And ye shall know that I am the Lord, when I have opened your graves, O my people, and brought you up out of your graves."

The promise to the redeemed of Israel who died in faith is also repeated in Hosea 13:14:

"I will ransom them from the power of the grave; I will redeem them from death: O death, I will be thy plagues; O grave, I will be thy destruction. . . ."

However, in all the promises of resurrection to the believing Israelites who died while yet looking forward to the Messiah, who would bring in the Kingdom, there is no mention of their bodies rising to meet the Messiah in the air. Their rewards are centered in the Kingdom context— Jerusalem, thrones in Israel, and in the new Jerusalem that will come down from God out of Heaven. Also, the time of the resurrection of the saints of Israel is prophesied to be at the time the Messiah came again to Jerusalem, and to the Temple. The resurrection of Israel is also prophesied to be after a time of great tribulation.

As we have already brought out, the resurrection of Israel will be after Michael and the armies of Heaven fight against Satan and his angels, and cast them out of the heavenlies. We refer again to Daniel 12:1-2:

"And at that time shall Michael stand up, the great prince which standeth for the children of thy people: and there shall be a time of trouble, such as never was since there was a nation even to that same time: and at that time thy people shall be delivered, every one that shall be found written in the book. And many of them that sleep in the dust of the earth shall awake, some to everlasting life, and some to shame and everlasting contempt."

The saints of Israel are to be resurrected after the time of Jacob's trouble. The redeemed of the church age are in no way referred to in this prophecy, because the Gentile church is not in view in the Old Testament. The prophets did not see the church age as they looked forward to the bringing in of the Kingdom age. It was hidden from their understanding, as Paul revealed in Ephesians 3:1-5. The people to be resurrected after the Tribulation period, as mentioned by Daniel, are called "thy people," meaning Daniel's people—Israel.

Resurrection of the Lost

We notice another kind of resurrection mentioned in Daniel 12:2—the resurrection of some to everlasting shame and contempt. Therefore, it is evident that not all of the people of Israel who lived before the cross will be raised to inherit the Kingdom. Some will be raised to suffer everlasting shame. The prophet Isaiah also wrote of the resurrection of the lost and their eternal destiny:

"For as the new heavens and the new earth, which I will make, shall remain before me, saith the Lord, so shall your seed and your name remain. And it shall come to pass, that from one new moon to another, and from one sabbath to another, shall all flesh come to worship before me, saith the Lord. And they shall go forth, and look upon the carcases of the men that have transgressed against me: for their worm shall not die, neither shall their fire be quenched; and they shall be an abhorring unto all flesh" (Isa. 66:22-24).

Isaiah brought his prophecy to a close with a graphic description of the resurrection of the lost, and their eternal punishment, as a warning to all who rejected God, and the way of salvation. But the Israelites were never in ignorance concerning the reality of Hell. Moses warned all who would turn away from God in Deuteronomy 32:21-24:

"They have moved me to jealousy . . . they have provoked me to anger with their vanities . . . a fire is kindled in mine anger, and shall burn unto the lowest hell . . . I will heap mischiefs upon them . . . They shall be burnt with hunger, and devoured with burning heat, and with bitter destruction. . . ."

There are <u>two references</u> to Hell in the first book of the Bible to be written, the book of Job. Even in the book of Proverbs, we find seven references to Hell and its consequences. David, by inspiration of God, proclaimed Hell for the lost just as strongly as he believed in resurrection and rewards for the redeemed. We read in Psalm 86:12-13:

"I will praise thee, O Lord my God, with all my heart: and I will glorify thy name for evermore. For great is thy mercy toward me: and thou hast delivered my soul from the lowest hell."

The prophet Isaiah warned the ungodly of Israel,

". . . hell hath enlarged herself, and opened her mouth without measure: and their glory, and their multitude, and their pomp, and he that rejoiceth, shall descend into it" (Isa. 5:14).

Ezekiel, Amos, Jonah, and Habakkuk also wrote about Hell. From the description afforded by the prophets in the Old Testament, we know that it will be a place of hunger, fire, distress, shame, contempt, darkness, and corruption. The lost will be raised in a body to stand before God and be judged. They will suffer degrees of these separate judgments in accordance with the sins they have committed in the flesh. The prophets wrote that there were places in Hell lower than other places, indicating degrees of punishment for the lost. In the last book of the Old Testament, in Malachi 4:1, we read this solemn warning:

> "For behold, the day cometh, that shall burn as
> an oven; and all the proud, yea, and all that do
> wickedly, shall be stubble: and the day that
> cometh shall burn them up. . . ."

From the Old Testament we learn that there will be a resurrection of both the just and the unjust. The redeemed will be raised to eternal life and rewards; the lost will be raised to eternal death and punishment. However, there is no clear distinction in the Old Testament as to the difference in time between the resurrection of the saved and the unsaved. While it is indicated that the resurrection of all who died before the cross will take place after the Great Tribulation at the literal coming of the Messiah, there is no clear evidence from the Old Testament that the raising of the saved and the raising of the lost will be separated by a period of time. But on the other hand, neither is there any scriptural evidence from the Old Testament that both the saved and the unsaved will be raised in one group at the same time. We are told only that the resurrection of the saved and the resurrection of the unsaved will occur after the time of Jacob's Trouble, the Great Tribulation, when the Messiah comes to bring in the Kingdom. We have to go to the New Testament for further differentiation between the two resurrections. It is in the New Testament where orders of resurrection is taught. Let us next discuss the souls of the Old Testament saints.

The Souls of the Old Testament Saints

There is no reason to doubt as to where the conscious self, the soul and spirit of a Christian, goes at death. Paul said in 2 Corinthians 5:8, ". . . to be absent from the body, and to be present with the Lord." A theologian may ignore this statement, but he cannot explain it away to mean soul sleeping. When a believer in Christ today dies, he goes to be with the Lord. Jesus Christ is in Heaven; therefore, when Christians die, they go to Heaven. Where the Scriptures in the New Testament refer to those who sleep in Jesus, they always refer to the bodies of Christians. The body sleeps in the dust of the earth until resurrection, but the soul and spirit are abundantly alive in the presence of Jesus Christ.

But what about the Old Testament saints? Did they go to Heaven in the presence of God at death?

There is no scriptural evidence in the Old Testament that the souls of the saints went to be with the Lord at death. Their souls and spirits were alive in a place described as Abraham's bosom. The place of the dead in the Old Testament is called Sheol or Hades. The saved went to a place of rest, while the lost went to a place of torment. Both compartments of Hades are described as being in the earth. In 1 Samuel 28:10-15, the spirit of Samuel is depicted as coming up out of the earth. The

Bible states emphatically that nothing sinful, unrighteous, or unholy can appear in the presence of God. The sinner must be cleansed from sin before entering the presence of God, and we read in Romans 3:23 that all have sinned. This includes the Old Testament saints.

The sprinkling of blood on the mercy seat that was over the Ark on the day of atonement was a practical demonstration to Israel that no one could enter the presence of God before his sins were cleansed by the blood. Paul wrote to the Hebrews that there was no remission of sins in the blood of bulls and goats sprinkled on the mercy seat in the tabernacle; because there is remission of sin only in the blood of Jesus Christ. We read in Romans 3:25 that Jesus Christ is that mercy seat (propitiation) that was set forth in type in the Old Testament. The Old Testament saints could not enter into the presence of God in Heaven until Christ died for their sins. Old Testament scriptures relating to redemption from sin through the coming Redeemer emphasize that He would be bruised for their iniquities and cut off for their transgressions and iniquities. But there was no cutting off from their sins until the Messiah came and died on the cross for them.

The priests and Levites taught the Israelites that their souls would rest in Abraham's bosom, and this teaching was verified by the Lord Jesus Christ in Luke 16:22:

> "And it came to pass, that the beggar died, and was carried by the angels into Abraham's bosom. . . ."

From *Fausset's Bible Dictionary* we read that in ancient Israel, it was the Jewish custom at feasts or the evening meal to recline on couches, each leaning on the left arm. The people at the feast would almost be leaning on each other's chest. To lean on the chest of the host was counted the highest place of honor. The Jews knew what Jesus meant when he said in John 1:18:

"No man hath seen God at any time; the only begotten Son, which is in the bosom of the Father, he hath declared him."

Jesus here was indicating His exalted position with the Father, because only one person can lie on the bosom of another. The artists' conceptions of the Last Supper always shows Jesus and the apostles sitting at the table with the Lord in the middle. But this was not the way it was at all. In Jewish tradition, they were all leaning on their left arms on a long couch, or on a mat in a circle on the floor. We read in John 13:21-26:

"When Jesus had thus said, he was troubled in spirit, and testified, and said, Verily, verily, I say unto you, that one of you shall betray me. Then the disciples looked one to another, doubting of whom he spake. Now there was leaning on Jesus' bosom one of his disciples, whom Jesus loved. Simon Peter therefore beckoned to him, that he should ask who it should be of whom he spake. He then lying on Jesus' breast said unto him, Lord, who is it? Jesus answered, He it is to whom I shall give a sop, when I have dipped it. And when he had dipped the sop, he gave it to Judas Iscariot. . . ."

The apostles were lying in a circle, or semi-circle, with the bread and the sop in the middle. John was occupying the honored position on Jesus' bosom. There are some sacrilegious people today who claim that Jesus was a homosexual because John was lying on His bosom, but these ridiculous blasphemers only reveal their ignorance. This was the traditional Jewish position for certain occasions.

Lazarus, the beggar, is described as leaning on Abraham's bosom, an honored position. The rich man who died in his sins is depicted as being in torment in Hell. Thus, the teaching of the priests and Levites that all who died in faith went to rest in the bosom of the father of faith, Abraham. All who died in unbelief and rebellion against God went to Hell.

It was the assurance of resurrection that made the prophets bold in their denunciation of sin as they called on the people of Israel to turn from their sin and turn back to God in faith and repentance. We read of the influence of the hope of resurrection on the preaching of the prophets in Hebrews 11:32-35:

> *"And what shall I more say? for the time would fail me to tell of Gedeon, and of Barak, and of Samson, and of Jephthae; of David also, and Samuel, and of the prophets; Who through faith subdued kingdoms, wrought righteousness, obtained promises, stopped the mouths of lions, Quenched the violence of fire, escaped the edge of the sword, out of weakness were made strong, waxed valiant in fight, turned to flight the armies of the aliens. Women received their dead raised to life again: and others were tortured, not accepting deliverance; **that they might obtain a better resurrection.**"*

<u>Acts 14:6</u>

The object of the Epistle.

The apostle knew that the Martyr's
death was soon to be his lot.

He has a great + deep desire
to see His beloved Timothy once
more.

He therefore wrote him to that
effect, greatly desiring to see thee
being mindful of thy tears, that
I may be filled with joy <u>(V1:4)</u>
Do thy diligence + come before
winter. <u>(4: 9, 11, 21)</u>

<u>V.6: That thou Rekindle</u>

<u>2ND Corn 1:</u>   God of all Comfort   Swan 2/1/98
           3   JOB   PSA23
           7:4-7,13   Church found now

Chap 1:-
<u>V.4 — in tribulation (when in distress)</u>

Dont drole   (accountant)

The subject of this Epistle

The apostle knew that the martyr's
death was soon to be his lot.
He has a great + deep desire to see
his beloved Tim once more.
He wrote him to that effect:
"greatly desiring to see thee"
being mindful of thy tears, that I may be
filled with joy (1:4) Do thy diligence
~~+ come before winter. 4:9, 11, 21~~
being uncertain how it might be with
himself, whether he should live or be
offered up before his arrival; he wrote
this letter with his final warnings
exhortations + instr.

10/13/97

John 20:20 — when they saw the Lord
"   12:20 -21 Sir we would see Jesus
Heb 2: 9.   But we see Jesus
John 5: 11 - 12

Chapter Four

Hades and Abraham's Bosom

In our preceding study, we discussed the resting place
of the souls of the Old Testament saints. The Hebrews
believed, and it is confirmed in Scripture, that the souls of
the dead went to Hades. Hades was divided into two
compartments: a place of torment where the wicked dead
went, and Abraham's bosom, a place of rest and peace
where the righteous went to wait for their resurrection.
Their resurrection was to come, as confirmed by
Scripture, when the Messiah came to bring in the
Kingdom.

The two compartments of Hades were separated by a
wide gulf, as related by Jesus in the account of Lazarus,
the beggar who rested in Abraham's bosom, and the rich
man who suffered in Hell.

The historian Josephus was a priest before he
became governor of Galilee. His given name was Joseph.
Josephus was the name the Romans gave him. He is best
known for his two works, *The Antiquities of the Jews*,
and *The Wars of the Jews*. But being a priest of Israel, he
was also a theologian, and in his "Discourse to the Greeks
Concerning Hades," Josephus set forth in great detail the
Jewish doctrine concerning Hell and Abraham's bosom.
We will not take time to quote all of it, but only those
portions necessary to shed more light on this subject:

"Now as to Hades, wherein the souls of the righteous and unrighteous are detained, it is necessary to speak of it. Hades is a place in the world not regularly finished; a subterraneous region, where the light of this world does not shine . . . there must be in it perpetual darkness. This region is allowed as a place of custody for souls, in which angels are appointed as guardians to them, who distribute to them temporary punishments, agreeable to every one's behavior and manners. In this region there is a certain place set apart, as a lake of unquenchable fire, wherein we suppose no one hath hitherto been cast; but it is prepared for a day afore-determined by God, in which one righteous sentence shall deservedly be passed upon all men. . . . The unjust shall be adjusted to this everlasting punishment . . . while the just shall obtain an incorruptible and never-fading kingdom. These are now indeed confined in Hades, but not in the same place where the unjust are confined. . . . There is one descent into this region, at whose gate we believe there stands an archangel with an host. . . . The just are guided to the right hand, and are led with hymns sung by the angels . . . unto a region of light, in which the just have dwelt from the beginning of the world . . . ever enjoying the prospect of the good things they see, and rejoice in the expectation of those new enjoyments. (In this place) there is no toil, no burning heat, no piercing cold, nor any briars; but the countenance of the fathers of the just, which they see, always smiles upon them, while they wait for that rest and

eternal new life in Heaven, which is to succeed this region. This place we call the bosom of Abraham. But as to the unjust, they are dragged by force to the left hand, by the angels allotted for punishment, as prisoners . . . to whom are sent angels appointed over them to reproach them and to threaten them with their terrible looks, and to thrust them still downward, drag them into the neighbourhood of Hell itself; who, when they are hard by it, continually hear the noise of it, and do not stand clear of the hot vapour itself; but when they have a nearer view of this spectacle, as of a terrible and exceeding great prospect of fire, they are struck with a fearful expectation of a future judgment . . . and not only so, but where they see the place of the fathers and of the just, even hereby are they punished; for a chaos deep and large is fixed between them; insomuch that a just man that hath compassion upon them, cannot be admitted, nor can one that is unjust, if he were bold enough to attempt it, pass over it. This is a discourse concerning Hades, wherein the souls of all men are confined until a proper season, which God hath determined, when he will make a resurrection of all men from the dead, not procuring a transmigration of souls from one body to another, but raising again those very bodies, which you Greeks, seeing to be dissolved, do not believe. . . . It must never be said of God that he is able to do some things, and unable to do others. We have therefore believed that the body will be raised again; for although it be dissolved, it is not perished; for the earth receives its remains, and preserves them; and while they are like seed, and are mixed among the more fruitful soil, they flourish, and what is sown is indeed bare grain; but at the mighty sound of God the Creator, it will sprout up, and be raised in a clothed and glorious condition . . . in a state of purity, and so as never to be destroyed any more . . . and when it hath clothed itself with that body, it will not be subject to misery. . . . All men, the just as well as the unjust, shall be brought before God the word, for to him hath the Father committed all judgment; said he, in order to fulfill the will of his Father, shall come a judge, whom we call Christ . . . allotting to the lovers of wicked works eternal punishment. To these belong the unquenchable fire, and that without end, and a certain fiery worm never dying, and not destroying the body . . . neither will sleep give ease to these men . . . death will not free them from their punishment, nor will the interceding prayers of their kindred profit them . . . but the just shall remember only their righteous actions, whereby they have attained the heavenly Kingdom, in which there is no sleep, no sorrow, no corruption, no care, no night, no day measured by time, no sun driven in its course along the circle of Heaven . . . no moon decreasing and increasing, or introducing a variety of seasons, nor will she then moisten the earth; no burning sun, no bear turning round the pole, no Orion to rise, no wandering of innumerable stars. The earth will not then be difficult to be passed over . . . nor will there be any fearful roaring of the sea, forbidding the passengers to walk on it: even that will be made easily passable to the just, though it will not be void of moisture; Heaven will not then be uninhabitable by men. . . . The earth will not be uncultivated, nor require too much labour of men, but will bring forth its fruits of its own accord . . . what God hath now concealed in silence will then be made manifest, what neither eye hath seen, nor ear hath heard, nor hath it entered into the heart of man, the things that God hath prepared for them that love him. . . . To God be glory and dominion for ever and ever. Amen."

We have quoted only a small portion of the dissertation of Josephus on Hades, Abraham's bosom, resurrection, and the earth to come. The reason we quoted as much as we did was to present the traditional, orthodox Jewish viewpoint on these subjects at the time of the first advent of Jesus Christ. Most of the views of Josephus are substantiated by Scripture, but we must not consider any of the writings of Josephus as inspired of God, except of course the scriptures which he quoted directly. Part of Josephus' description of the resurrection of the just and their glorified bodies agrees almost word for word with Paul's remarks about resurrection in the fifteenth chapter of 1 Corinthians. Inasmuch as Josephus did believe that Jesus was the Christ, and the Romans turned over to him all the religious and historical documents in the empire, it is quite possible that he had copies of some of Paul's epistles.

It is easy to see, from the dissertation of Josephus on Hades, where the doctrine of the Roman Catholic Church on Purgatory originated. However, the historian contended that the prayers of the saints on earth had no effect on the tormented state of those in Hades. The description that Josephus gave of Hades, with the wide gulf separating the place of the just and the unjust, is seemingly scriptural. His account of resurrection and the glorified body is also accurate and in accordance with the Bible, and his description of the New Earth and the New Heavens is remarkably in accord with the revelation given to John. We also have no fault to find with this ex-priest's account of the last judgment. He said that the lost dead would be resurrected to stand before God the Word, the Christ of Whom God has committed all judgment, to be judged for their deeds. He did not say the just would stand before the Great Judge at this judgment.

The main difference between the dissertation of Josephus on Hades and the Pauline epistles is that Josephus held to the traditional Jewish position that salvation was by works, and that the souls of the just were still in Abraham's bosom in the Paradise compartment of Hades. But we should remember that Josephus was a Pharisee, a priest of Judaism, he had no real conception of the Gentile church age, or the atoning work of Jesus Christ on the cross. The status of the Old Testament dead—both the just and the unjust—since the crucifixion of Christ is adequately explained in the book *Where Are the Dead?* by Karl Sabiers. Since we cannot improve upon this explanation, we quote it for you:

> *"The Scripture reveals that since Christ's resurrection and ascension to the Father in Heaven, the section known as 'Abraham's bosom' or 'Paradise' in Hades, is no longer the abode for the spirits of the righteous dead. Before*

Christ's resurrection and ascension, Hades or Sheol, the spirit-world, is represented as being below, and into it all the dead, both saved and lost, are said to have descended. Following Christ's resurrection and ascension, Hades is never mentioned as the abode of redeemed spirits. After the ascension of Christ, the spirits of the righteous instead of 'descending' are spoken of as going up. In 2 Corinthians, the twelfth chapter, Paul relates his experiences. He tells of being 'caught up to the third Heaven . . . caught up into Paradise.' According to this account of New Testament Scripture, 'Paradise' and the 'third Heaven' have the same location. . . . When did this change take place? The Scripture says in Ephesians 4:8-10 that before Christ ascended up into Heaven, 'He descended first into the lower parts of the earth.' Now then, when Christ ascended did He go alone? NO! He brought a multitude with Him. He took the waiting spirits of the Paradise section of Hades with Him. The Scripture says when He ascended up on high He led captivity captive. The marginal reading is, 'He led a multitude of captives.' We are also positive that the righteous dead are no longer in Hades, because we know that they are with Christ where He is. Paul said in Philippians 1:23 that he desired to 'depart to be with Christ.' And in 2 Corinthians 5:6-8, Paul uses strong words in expressing his confidence that to be 'absent from the body' in death, is to be 'present with the Lord,' therefore they must be where Christ is. Now then, where is Christ? Is He in Hades? NO! We know that the Lord is not in

Hades, because the Scripture says of Christ in Acts 2:27 that His soul was not left in Hades. Where is He then? Dozens of other scriptures tell us that He has ascended into the Heavens and is at the right hand of God. Inasmuch as the departed spirits of the righteous are present with the Lord, they must be there where He is—up in Heaven—not down in the 'section' of Hades known as 'Abraham's bosom' or 'Paradise.' These conclusions definitely prove that 'Paradise,' the abode of the righteous, is no longer in Hades, but that since the ascension of Christ, the abode of the righteous is 'with the Lord.' Jesus plainly declared that Sheol-Hades will not prevail against the true church. Matthew 16:18, 'And I say also unto thee, That thou art Peter, and upon this rock I will build my church: and the gates of Hell (Hades) shall not prevail against it.' Sheol-Hades will never be the abiding place of any true saint of this age. The reason the Old Testament righteous went to Sheol-Hades was because their sins were not yet put away (Heb. 10:4). But Hebrews 9:26 says, 'But now once in the end of the world (ages) He (Christ) hath appeared to put away sin by the sacrifice of Himself.' Therefore when the sins of the Old Testament righteous were 'put away' by Christ's sacrifice on Calvary, they could enter into the very presence of God as do the spirits of the righteous of this age. The spirits of the lost, the wicked dead, still go to Hades into 'the place of torment.' No change in their abode has been revealed in Scripture. They are still in Hades, and all the spirits of the unrighteous who shall die in the future will also go there. This is true because the 'Great White Throne' judgment at which the wicked are to appear, we read in Revelation 20:13, Hell (Hades) delivered up the dead. This proves that Hades is still the abode of unrighteousness, and it will be until the time of the 'Great White Throne' judgment—which is future. At that time the spirits of the wicked will be brought up out of Hades, not out of some other place."

We trust our review of the two accounts concerning the places of the dead has helped to clear up your understanding: one by Josephus outlining the orthodox Jewish position from the Old Testament, and why the souls of the righteous dead no longer go to Hades, as explained by Dr. Sabiers from the New Testament.

There is one other matter which we should clear up before we proceed in our study of Rapture and resurrection, and this concerns Jesus' remark to the thief who called upon His Name from the cross. Jesus said to the thief, " . . . *To day shalt thou be with me in paradise."* This is found in Luke 23:43, the first place where the word is mentioned. It is not a Hebrew word, or even a Greek word. It is a Persian word which means a beautiful garden, a place of quiet and peace. We get our word "park" from "paradise." This means that the thief who called upon the Name of Jesus Christ and was saved must have been a Gentile. If Jesus had said to this man, "Today thou shalt be with me in Abraham's bosom," it probably would not have meant a thing to him. Our Lord's selecting the Gentile word "paradise" indicates that He was dying for the sins of the world, not just for the sins of Israel.

In 2 Corinthians 12:4 Paul said that he was caught up to Paradise, so he must have seen the souls of those who died in faith, and this was one of the most moving experiences of the apostle's life. Paul said that it was such a glorious sight that God gave him a thorn in the flesh just so that he would keep his feet on the ground, and think of the needs of others instead of having his mind always on the things of Heaven.

This is a marvelous assurance to those who have loved ones who have died in the faith of the Lord Jesus. They are in Paradise, a beautiful place of peace and quiet. Their troubles are over, and they are waiting to return with Jesus for their glorified bodies. This marvelous revelation should also inspire Christians to renew their efforts to get their friends and loved ones saved while there is yet time.

Chapter Five

Resurrection In the Gospels

All resurrection promises in the Old Testament are centered in the coming of the Redeemer, the Savior, the Messiah. Without the coming of Christ, all those in the Old Testament who died in faith would have died in vain. Likewise, without the resurrection of Jesus Christ from the grave, the hope of all Christians for eternal life would be in vain. Paul forthrightly declared the necessity of the literal resurrection of the body of Christ from the grave in 1 Corinthians 15:13-14:

"But if there be no resurrection of the dead, then is Christ not risen: And if Christ be not risen, then is our preaching vain, and your faith is also vain."

Jesus Christ declared Himself to be the only hope of mankind in a literal resurrection. He said, as recorded in John 11:25-26:

". . . I am the resurrection, and the life: he that believeth in me, though he were dead, yet shall he live: And whosoever liveth and believeth in me shall never die. . . ."

When Jesus was born of the virgin Mary, the nation

of Israel was divided into three main groups: the Sadducees, the Pharisees, and the lower class. The Sadducees were the upper class, composed mostly of the wealthy—the land owners and the richer merchants. The Sadducees were mostly agnostic in their belief toward God. Even some of the higher priests were included within the membership of this sect. The Sadducees' heaven was here on earth, and they denied the existence of angels, a future life, and the resurrection. We read in Matthew 22:23:

"The same day came to him the Sadducees, which say that there is no resurrection. . . ."

The second division of Israel according to theology was the Pharisees. The Pharisees were of the middle class. They were very patriotic and prided themselves on being keepers of the law and traditions of Israel. Therefore, being students of the Scriptures, they stoutly believed in the resurrection of the dead. Because they believed in the resurrection, some of the Pharisees became disciples of Jesus when He demonstrated His power over death in the raising of the dead. However, the majority of the Pharisees rejected Jesus as the promised Messiah, and it was their influence over the people that led to the crucifixion of Jesus Christ.

The lower class, which comprised the vast majority of Israel at that time, were too busy earning their daily bread to become involved in politics or religion. Most of them were honest, hard-working people, who did the best they could to provide for their families, honor the law, worship God, and go up to Jerusalem at least once a year at the time of Passover. It was from the lower class that Jesus won most of His disciples.

Because all the Old Testament teachings on resurrection looked forward to the coming of the Messiah, the miracles of Jesus in the raising of the dead, and His teachings on this subject, comprised an important part of His earthly ministry. His declarations that He was the resurrection and the life was followed by a visible demonstration to prove that He was the Redeemer Who had come to raise the dead. After Jesus professed to Martha that He was the One Who was sent by God to bring the dead back to life, we read the account of what happened next in John 11:41-46:

"Then they took away the stone from the place where the dead was laid. And Jesus lifted up his eyes, and said, Father, I thank thee that thou hast heard me. And I knew that thou hearest me always: but because of the people which stand by I said it, that they may believe that thou hast sent me. And when he thus had spoken, he cried with a loud voice, Lazarus, come forth. And he that was dead came forth, bound hand and foot with graveclothes; and his face was bound about with a napkin. Jesus saith unto them, Loose him, and let him go. Then many of the Jews which came to Mary, and had seen the things which Jesus did, believed on him. But some of them went their ways to the Pharisees, and told them what things Jesus had done."

Lazarus had been dead for several days, and his body already was in the process of decaying. Yet Jesus restored the soul and the spirit to the body, and the dead man lived. Another account of Jesus raising the dead is recorded in Luke 8:49-56, where the Lord restored to life the dead body of Jairus' daughter. However, these miracles in raising the dead were mere signs of Christ's power over death, and not literal demonstrations of resurrection. Neither the daughter of Jairus nor Lazarus was raised in a glorified body. It is evident from Scripture that they lived out their normal life span, and then died a natural death. We read in 1 Corinthians 15:21-23:

"For since by man came death, by man came also the resurrection of the dead. For as in Adam all die, even so in Christ shall all be made alive. But every man in his own order: Christ the firstfruits; afterward they that are Christ's at his coming."

Jesus Christ was the first to be raised in an incorruptible and immortal body. There will be no other person raised in a glorified body until Christ's return. Many Christians are concerned about what happened in Matthew 27:50-54:

"Jesus, when he had cried again with a loud voice, yielded up the ghost. And, behold, the veil of the temple was rent in twain from the top to the bottom; and the earth did quake, and the rocks rent; And the graves were opened; and many bodies of the saints which slept arose, And came out of the graves after his resurrection, and went into the holy city, and appeared unto many. Now when the centurion, and they that were with him, watching Jesus, saw the earthquake, and those things that were done, they feared greatly, saying, Truly this was the Son of God."

Jesus Christ was resurrected in a glorified body, but Matthew does not call the appearance of the saints in a body a resurrection. This probably was a localized miracle for the benefit of Israel, to again prove to the Jews that Jesus Christ was the Son of God, the promised Messiah. Not all the saints arose—only some in the graveyard in the vicinity of Jerusalem. This miracle is recorded only in Matthew, indicating that it was a sign to the Jews, and it is nowhere else mentioned in the Bible. What happened to the bodies of the saints that arose after the resurrection of Jesus and appeared to many in Jerusalem is not known. It is not necessary that we do know. Inasmuch as Jesus Christ has the power to restore a dead, decaying body to life, He could have brought the bodies of the saints in the graveyard at Jerusalem back to life for five minutes, an hour, a day, or whatever length of time it was needed to prove that He had risen with the power of resurrection over all death. This particular incident was another miracle to show Israel that if the nation would receive Jesus as Messiah, all the saints would be resurrected, and the promised Kingdom would be brought in at that time.

We may wonder about the translation of Enoch and Elijah, in light of Paul's statement that Jesus Christ is the only one to this date who has been resurrected in a glorified body. Enoch was translated before the flood, and Elijah was taken up to Heaven in a fiery, whirling celestial vehicle about 1000 B.C. Both men had to be changed in order to go up into the Heavens, but nowhere in Scripture is their translation, or changing from earth to Heaven, spoken of as resurrection. Their bodies did not decay, and we read in Hebrews 11:5 that Enoch did not see death. The bodies of the Christians who are alive at the Rapture will be translated in like manner.

Another somewhat perplexing statement made by Jesus about resurrection is found in Matthew 22:23-30. The Sadducees, who did not believe in resurrection, attempted to trick the Lord by asking Him about a hypothetical incident where a woman had married seven brothers. It was all according to the law. Her first husband died, and she married the next brother, and on down the line until all seven had died, and she had become the wife of each one in succession. All seven brothers and the wife had died in faith, so the Sadducees wanted to know whose wife the woman would be in the resurrection. Jesus replied in verses 29 and 30:

> *"Jesus answered and said unto them, Ye do err, not knowing the scriptures, nor the power of God. For in the resurrection they neither marry, nor are given in marriage, but are as the angels of God in heaven."*

Jesus did not say that angels are sexless. It seems apparent that the reason there are no marriages within the angelic order of God is that there are no female angels. Before the flood, the angels of God saw the daughters of men, and took wives of them (Gen. 6). Angels are always referred to in the masculine gender in the Bible, and when seen of others, they are called "men." The angels of God before the flood who tooks wives from among men, left their heavenly estate, their created order. They no longer belonged to the angelic order of Heaven. We believe these are the angels referred to in Jude 6:

> *". . . the angels which kept not their first estate, but left their own habitation, he hath reserved in everlasting chains under darkness unto the judgment of the great day."*

It is usually interpreted that Paul meant in 1 Corinthians 13:13 that the saved will be known in Heaven even as they are known on earth. But what identifies the individual? Is it outward physical appearance, or the personality? Is our physical appearance our identity, or do what we think, how we act, what we say, and our feelings and emotions identify us more? Man looks on the outward appearance, but God looks upon the inward man. To think we are going to have a certain physical appearance, or have sex in Heaven in order to be happy, is to limit the power of God like the Sadducees did. Jesus assured the Christians that the entire matter is in God's hands, and whatever is for His eternal honor and glory, that is what the Creator will do. So as Paul said, eye has not seen, ear heard, or entered into the mind of man what God has in store for those who love Him. We can be sure that whatever replaces sex in the resurrection will be at least a million times better. Sex was given to man for the purpose of procreation, and procreation ends in resurrection. The Scriptures say that the resurrection body will be a spiritual body—we will be known by our spiritual identity more than our physical appearance.

The Old Testament teaching concerning the resurrection of both the just and the unjust was verified by Jesus in John 5:28-29:

"Marvel not at this: for the hour is coming, in the which all that are in the graves shall hear his voice, And shall come forth; they that have done good, unto the resurrection of life; and they that have done evil, unto the resurrection of damnation."

In this scripture, Jesus seemingly grouped the resurrection of the saved and the unsaved in one general resurrection, as presented in the Old Testament. However, in other teachings of Jesus on the subject, we begin to see a division between the two groups. For example, we read in Luke 14:13-14:

> *"But when thou makest a feast, call the poor, the maimed, the lame, the blind: And thou shalt be blessed: for they cannot recompense thee: for thou shalt be recompensed at the resurrection of the just."*

In other scriptures, Jesus made references to the resurrection of the lost and the saved as being two separate events, or the resurrection of one group is mentioned without making reference to the other.

Some believe that the Rapture of the church is revealed in the Lord's parable of the ten virgins; however, it is our understanding that there is no reference to resurrection in this parable, or to the church. Quoting Dr. William Pettingill:

> *"The parable of the ten virgins has no direct reference to Christians of any 'class'; it refers to professing Jewish believers and some mere professors, 'having not the spirit.' Any teaching is mischevious which divides born-again ones into 'classes.' The Rapture is for all who belong to the Lord, and He 'knoweth them that are his.' "*

The greatest teaching on the resurrection by Jesus was by and through His own resurrection. He predicted that He would die and be raised again. We read His words in Matthew 12:40:

"For as Jonas was three days and three nights in the whale's belly; so shall the Son of man be three days and three nights in the heart of the earth."

He arose again the third day to prove to man that there was a resurrection from the dead, and He said in John 14:19, *". . . because I live, ye shall live also."* He was seen of above five hundred witnesses. God raised Him up to prove to the world that He had offered a payment for sins, that through faith in Him men could be raised in a glorified body and stand before the Creator. It was the resurrection of Jesus Christ that inspired the greatest message to mortal man ever written:

". . . when this corruptible shall have put on incorruption, and this mortal shall have put on immortality, then shall be brought to pass the saying that is written, Death is swallowed up in victory, O death, where is thy sting? O grave, where is thy victory? The sting of death is sin; and the strength of sin is the law. But thanks be to God, which giveth us the victory through our Lord Jesus Christ. Therefore, my beloved brethren, be ye stedfast, unmoveable, always abounding in the work of the Lord, forasmuch as ye know that your labour is not in vain in the Lord" (1 Cor. 15:54-58).

Chapter Six

Resurrection In the
Book of Acts

When the Sadducees were attempting to discredit the teachings of Jesus on resurrection, our Lord's reply to them was:

". . . as touching the resurrection of the dead, have ye not read that which was spoken unto you by God, saying, I am the God of Abraham, and the God of Isaac, and the God of Jacob? God is not the God of the dead, but of the living" (Matt. 22:31-32).

Every saint from Abel to this present hour is living, and Jesus Christ, through His death for sin and resurrection from the grave, gave assurance to all men everywhere that there is a glorious, immortal, and eternal life for all who receive God's only begotten Son as Lord and Savior. Any preacher who denies the literal resurrection of Jesus Christ is the most effective agent that Satan has in the world. The Devil does not want us to believe in a future resurrection. If men and women do not believe in an existence beyond the grave, then the guiding philosophy of the world becomes: eat, drink, and be merry, for tomorrow we die. It is incomprehensible to even imagine what it would be like to live in a world where there was no hope of life beyond the death of the physical body.

The good news that the early disciples preached was that the Savior had come; He had died for man's iniquity; He had risen from the grave and loosed the bonds of death. We read from Peter's sermon to Israel in Acts 2:22-24:

> *"Ye men of Israel, hear these words; Jesus of Nazareth, a man approved of God among you by miracles and wonders and signs, which God did by him in the midst of you, as ye yourselves also know: Him, being delivered by the determinate counsel and foreknowledge of God, ye have taken, and by wicked hands have crucified and slain: Whom God hath raised up, having loosed the pains of death. . . ."*

The primary message of the church is that there is reconciliation to God, and resurrection of the body, through faith in Jesus Christ. The Devil's agents attempted to silence the message of the disciples for one reason, and that reason was, as explained in Acts 4:2, they were

> *". . . grieved that they taught the people, and preached through Jesus the resurrection from the dead."*

Paul was likewise persecuted: beaten with stripes, thrown to the beasts, put into dungeons, and finally executed, for preaching the gospel of resurrection through faith in Jesus Christ. He startled and offended the philosophers, mathematicians, and scientists of Greece with his preaching, as we read in Acts 17:18:

"Then certain philosophers of the Epicureans, and the Stoicks, encountered him. And some said, What will this babbler say? . . . He seemeth to be a setter forth of strange gods: because he preached unto them Jesus, and the resurrection."

But Paul never changed his message. In spite of ridicule and the scars on his body as a constant reminder, he preached to both Jews and Gentiles the promise of eternal life and the resurrection of the dead through faith in Jesus Christ. When he returned to Jerusalem, the Sanhedrin plotted to kill him, because as the apostle said in Acts 23:6, *". . . of the hope and resurrection of the dead am I called in question."*

As Paul stood before Felix, the Roman governor, to be judged, he said:

". . . this I confess unto thee, that after the way which they call heresy, so worship I the God of my fathers, believing all things which are written in the law and in the prophets: And have hope toward God, which they themselves also allow, that there shall be a resurrection of the dead, both of the just and unjust. And herein do I exercise myself, to have always a conscience void of offence toward God, and toward men . . ." (Acts 24:14-16).

Paul confessed that he was guilty as charged of preaching the resurrection of the dead through faith in Jesus Christ. He said that he could not stand before God or look men in their faces unless he faithfully proclaimed this message, because it was the hope of the world. Just before Paul was executed, he wrote to Timothy to be faithful in preaching the resurrection of the dead (2 Tim. 2:18-19). And in the last few words to come from the apostle's pen, he wrote:

> ". . . *the Lord shall deliver me from every evil work, and will preserve me unto his heavenly kingdom: to whom be glory for ever and ever. Amen"* (2 Tim. 4:18).

Likewise, the blessed assurance of eternal life with Jesus Christ and resurrection at His coming again have sprung from the lips of Christian martyrs as they were nailed to the crosses, thrown to the lions, or burned at the stake.

Chapter Seven

Resurrection In the Epistles

As we have already brought out in this study, the Old Testament saints were assured of their own rewards in resurrection. We read in Hebrews 11:26 that Moses was assured of his reward; Job looked forward to his lot in the resurrection, and so did Daniel, and all the others. The twelve apostles of Jesus continually plagued Him with questions about their own rewards in the kingdom. They reminded Him on one occasion that they had forsaken everything to follow Him. He finally answered in Matthew 18:28-29:

> *"And Jesus said unto them, Verily I say unto you, that ye which have followed me, in the regeneration when the Son of man shall sit in the throne of his glory, ye also shall sit upon twelve thrones, judging the twelve tribes of Israel. And every one that hath forsaken houses, or brethren, or sisters, or father, or mother, or wife, or children, or lands, for my name's sake, shall receive an hundredfold, and shall inherit everlasting life."*

The promise of rewards by Jesus was for the Jewish disciples at that time. Certainly, anything that we give up for Jesus will be repaid a hundredfold, but the promise of rewards given by Jesus to the Jewish disciples was related to the regeneration, when the Lord comes back to sit upon the throne of David. Their rewards were to be related to the covenant promises to Israel. The greatest rewards were to go to the twelve apostles in the regeneration, and the word for regeneration means literally the time of renewing this present earth—the Kingdom age, or the Millennium. But we read in Ephesians 2:12 that the Gentiles are aliens to the commonwealth of Israel and strangers to the covenants of promise. The resurrection of Israel and the giving of rewards is related to the coming of the Messiah, the King, in great glory. In Revelation 19 we are told of the coming of Jesus Christ as King of kings and Lord of lords. The Antichrist and his armies are destroyed. In Revelation 20, Satan is bound for a thousand years, Israel is restored to the land, and we read in Revelation 20:4: *"And I saw thrones, and they sat upon them, and judgment was given unto them. . . ."* These are the twelve thrones promised the apostles.

But what of the resurrection of the Christian, and his rewards? Like the twelve apostles, Job, Daniel, Abraham, and the saints of the Old Testament, do we not have a right to know when our resurrection will come, and what our estate will be in the eternal Kingdom of God? The church, meaning that body of all born-again believers during the dispensation of God's sovereign grace, is a separate entity within the entire family of God. James acknowledged this in Acts 15:14-16:

"Simeon hath declared how God at the first did visit the Gentiles, to take out of them a people for his name. And to this agree the words of the prophets; as it is written, After this I will return,

*and will build again the tabernacle of David,
which is fallen down; and I will build again the
ruins thereof, and I will set it up. "*

This is one thing the Scriptures emphatically declare
concerning the church. The church age, the calling out of
a people from the Gentiles for the glory of God, will end
when God again begins to restore the tabernacle of David.
Whether we interpret the church age as beginning at
Pentecost, with the conversion of Paul, or at Acts 28:28,
everyone should agree that it will have a definite end.

And so, what of this great company of Gentiles saved
through faith in Jesus Christ unto resurrection and
eternal life? What of this great body called the church, in
which there is neither male nor female, Jew nor Greek?

In seeking special information about the resurrection
and rewards of Christians, it seems reasonable that we
should look in the books of the Bible that were written
especially to the church. To Paul was given the revelation
concerning the church of the dispensation of grace, and it
was Paul who wrote specifically about Christian evan-
gelism, Christian service, church government, rewards,
and resurrection. Certainly, there is nothing in the
writings of Paul to the church that contradicts any of the
covenants and promises of God to saints of any former
age. God simply chose Paul to reveal to Christians their
calling, service, and heritage. We read again in Ephesians
3:1-5:

*"For this cause I Paul, the prisoner of Jesus
Christ for you Gentiles, If ye have heard of the
dispensation of the grace of God which is given
me to you-ward: How that by revelation he
made known unto me the mystery . . . Which in*

*other ages was not made known unto the sons of
men. . . ."*

We notice that Paul said this mystery was not made
known unto the "sons of men" in other ages. He did not
say "sons of God" of former ages, because from Adam to
Jesus Christ there was no son of God from among men.
Sonship with God was restored through adoption by a
new birth into God's family.

Jesus Christ revealed the entire scope of resurrection.
Paul revealed to the Christians their order within God's
entire program for resurrection. Jesus Christ separated
the resurrection of the saved from the resurrection of the
unsaved. Paul separated the resurrection and translation
of the church of the dispensation of grace from the
resurrection of the redeemed of former ages. The apostle
of the church wrote in 1 Corinthians 15:20-23:

*"But now is Christ risen from the dead, and
become the firstfruits of them that slept. For
since by man came death, by man came also the
resurrection of the dead. For as in Adam all die,
even so in Christ shall all be made alive. But
every man in his own **order**: Christ the firstfruits;
afterward they that are Christ's at his coming."*

Jesus Christ is the firstfruits of the first resurrection,
the resurrection of the just. No one since Jesus Christ has
been raised from the dead in an immortal body. After
Christ, the resurrection of all the saved will be at His
coming again. However, Paul placed an important qualification upon the resurrection of the saved at the second
coming. He said, *"But every man in his own order. . . ."*
The word for "order" in the Greek text is *tagma*, meaning

rank or company. The word is used in the Septuagint to refer to soldiers in rank passing in review. Soldiers still pass in review in rank and order, to be judged for appearance, drill precision, and obedience to orders. Afterward, special commendations are made by the judge. Christians are told that they will stand before the Judgment Seat of Christ. The Judgment Seat at which Christians will stand is called in the Greek the "Bema Seat," meaning it will be a judgment according to works, and they will be rewarded according to the service they have rendered. The service of Christians is different from the saved of former ages. Paul said in Ephesians 3:9-12 that God had determined before the world that the church would reign with Christ in heavenly places. Thus, the heritage of the church is also different. The Bible states emphatically that the church age will end at a definite time; therefore, no Christians will be left in the world when this time limit expires. For these reasons, the church, all born-again believers saved during the dispensation of grace, will be taken out of this world in one body, one company. In one order, or rank, Christians will appear before the Bema Seat to receive rewards. These rewards that Christians will receive will enhance their ability to serve God in heavenly places for all eternity.

As we read in 1 Thessalonians 4:13-17, the bodies of Christians who are at home with the Lord will be raised first, then those Christians who are alive at the exact moment the church age expires, will be changed in body and caught up with the resurrected saints in one company to meet Jesus Christ up in the air. Paul speaks of the resurrection and translation of the church as taking place in one day. He said in 2 Timothy 4:8:

"Henceforth there is laid up for me a crown of

*righteousness, which the Lord, the righteous judge, shall give me at that **day**: and not to me only, but unto all them also that love his appearing."*

Concerning the realm of resurrection as applying specifically to Christians, the Apostle Paul found it difficult to find words in human language that were adequate to express the future glory of the members of Christ's body. In Ephesians 2:4-7 Paul indicates that our resurrection glory is to be an extending magnification process to continue forever, bringing new joy with each passing moment:

"But God, who is rich in mercy, for his great love wherewith he loved us, Even when we were dead in sins, hath quickened us together with Christ, (by grace ye are saved;) And hath raised us up together, and made us sit together in heavenly places in Christ Jesus: That in the ages to come he might shew the exceeding riches of his grace in his kindness toward us through Christ Jesus."

In this body of corruptible flesh, God is limited concerning the blessings He can bestow upon us. But when Christians receive their glorified spiritual bodies, God will show us without end the riches of His grace because of His great love for those who received Jesus Christ, God's only begotten Son, as Lord and Savior. And how rich is God? Paul reckoned in Romans 11:33:

"O the depth of the riches of the wisdom and knowledge of God! how unsearchable are his judgments, and his ways past finding out!"

The Pauline epistles depict resurrection for the Christian as a door to the vault of the universe, the unfathomable riches of God.

Chapter Eight

The Rapture of the Church

In the preceding chapter we discussed the Christian hope of resurrection, and why we believe the resurrection and translation of the church will be a separate and secret event. And this brings us to a detailed biblical description of the Rapture. Once again we remind you that Rapture means the catching away of the church from the earth at the end of this present age. God's promise of resurrection and translation of believers of the church age was committed to the Apostle Paul, and it is recorded in 1 Thessalonians 4:13-18. We believe that it would be beneficial to our understanding of the Rapture to study the Christian hope of resurrection verse by verse:

"But I would not have you to be ignorant, brethren, concerning them which are asleep, that ye sorrow not, even as others which have no hope" (vs. 13).

God wants every Christian to be informed concerning His promise of a future resurrection. He does not want Christians to remain in a period of extended grief over loved ones who have died in the faith of Jesus Christ. God realizes that it is natural for us to experience sorrow at the separation of loved ones because of physical death, but

He also wants us to remember that He has promised that to be absent from the body is to be at home with the Lord. He has also promised a future resurrection of the body, and we read in Romans 4:21 that what God has promised, He is able to perform. The word "alseep" refers to the Christian body, never to the soul and spirit. The soul is at home with the Lord until the resurrection of the body. As Jesus Christ said, God is not the God of the dead. He is the God of the living.

> *"For if we believe that Jesus died and rose again, even so them also which sleep in Jesus will God bring with him"* (vs. 14).

A requirement for Jew and Gentile to be partakers in the Rapture is to believe that Jesus Christ, God's only begotten Son, died for the sins of the world, and that He arose from the grave and ascended back to the Father to await His second coming. Romans 10:9 declares:

> *". . . if thou shalt confess with thy mouth the Lord Jesus, and shalt believe in thine heart that God hath raised him from the dead, thou shalt be saved."*

Paul did not say anything about the hope of the Old Testament saints who died looking forward to the coming Redeemer. He did not say anything about the Tribulation saints, or those who would live on earth during the Millennium. He spoke specifically to Christians of this dispensation. He said that all who died in the faith that Jesus paid the penalty for sin, and that He rose again from the grave, their souls were with Jesus and their bodies were asleep in the ground to await Christ's returns The spirit and soul of all Christians who have died will return with Him. Paul says these ". . . *will God bring with him.*"

> *"For this we say unto you by the word of the Lord, that we which are alive and remain unto the coming of the Lord shall not prevent them which are alseep"* (vs. 15).

There will be Christians alive on the earth when the Lord returns for His church. The word "prevent" in the Greek text is *phthano*, which means to go before, or to be at the head of the line. It has been changed to "precede" in the New Scofield Bible. We also note that Paul says "by the word of the Lord" He is coming back. Jesus said, ". . . *if I go away, I will come again.*" To deny that Jesus is coming back is the same thing as calling Him a liar. The question is not, "Is He coming?" but rather, "When is He coming?"

> *"For the Lord himself shall descend from heaven with a shout, with the voice of the archangel, and with the trump of God: and the dead in Christ shall rise first"* (vs. 16).

Jesus said in John 5:25-27:

> *"Verily, verily, I say unto you, The hour is coming, and now is, when the dead shall hear the voice of the Son of God: and they that hear shall live. For as the Father hath life in himself; so hath he given to the Son to have life in himself; And hath given him authority to execute judgment also, because he is the Son of man."*

When Jesus raised Lazarus from the dead, we read that He *". . . cried with a loud voice, Lazarus, come forth"* (John 11:43). Jesus called the name of Lazarus. If Jesus had not specifically mentioned the name of Lazarus, then it is quite possible that every person who had died, from the time of Adam, would have risen from the grave. And Jesus said that the time is coming when He will call out to all the living dead, those who are saved, to come forth from the grave. He also said that He would execute judgment to the unsaved, but the Lord indicated that the resurrection of the saved and the resurrection of the unsaved would be separate events. Paul said that when Jesus returns, He will come with a shout. The word in the Greek is *keleusma*, which means a command. Just as Jesus shouted at Lazarus to come forth from the grave, He will shout to all who have died in faith. Every Christian who has died in faith will spring forth from the grave. Soul, spirit, and body will be reunited. Paul also said that Christ would return with the trump of God. This trumpet is not the seventh trumpet of Revelation 11:15. The trumpet at the Rapture is a trumpet of blessing. The seventh trumpet of Revelation is a trumpet of judgment upon the unsaved. The trumpet at the Rapture heralds an event that will take place in a moment, in the twinkling of an eye. The seventh trumpet of Revelation heralds several events that will require several months to consummate. When Jesus Christ shouts, the bodies of Christians will spring from the grave. When the trumpet sounds, they will rise in the air. Trumpets in Israel were used to assemble the people. Christ shouts to command the dead to spring forth, and the trumpet sounds to assemble the church in the air. Paul also informed us that the dead in Christ would rise first.

"Then we which are alive and remain shall be caught up together with them in the clouds, to meet the Lord in the air: and so shall we ever be with the Lord."

As the trumpet sounds, the Christians who are alive at this time will be caught up immediately with the resurrected Christians, and then all will be caught up together to meet the Lord Jesus Christ in the air. And how far up in the air will Jesus Christ be? The Scriptures do not say. We would venture to say not over a hundred miles because our air, or atmosphere, does not extend beyond that distance. The words "caught up" are expressed in the Greek with one word, *harpazo*, which means literally to hurriedly grasp up in your arms and carry off. In the Latin the words mean rapture, as a bridegroom carrying off his bride. The Christians who are asleep in Jesus will be raised in an eternal, glorified body. The Christians who are alive will be changed. The change will take place faster than changing a suit of clothes. Paul said in 1 Corinthians 14:51-52:

"Behold, I shew you a mystery; We shall not all sleep [some will be living], *but we shall all be changed, In a moment, in the twinkling of an eye, at the last trump: for the trumpet shall sound, and the dead shall be raised incorruptible, and we shall be changed."*

Paul said that the entire body of Christians would be caught up "in the clouds." There is much controversy as to what type of clouds are meant here. Some believe that they are clouds of saints as referred to in Hebrews 12:1, *"Wherefore seeing we also are encompassed about with so great a cloud of witnesses. . . ."*

But the word for cloud in Hebrews 12:1 means an indefinite mass, while the Greek word used for clouds in 1 Thessalonians 4:17 means definite objects. These could be regular clouds, or they could be celestial transportation ships like the cloudy pillar that led the children of Israel in the wilderness, or like the one that stood before the tabernacle. We notice the wording again, *". . . caught up . . . in the clouds."* Then Paul added, *". . . and so shall we ever be with the Lord."* The church is referred to as the espoused, or bride, of Christ. The church is also called the "body of Christ." It is natural, therefore, that from the time of the Rapture, all Christians will be forever with Jesus.

"Wherefore comfort one another with these words" (vs. 18).

The promise of the resurrection and translation of the Christian is our blessed comfort, and when times of trial and testing come, we remind each other of this blessed hope. Paul said we should comfort each other with the promise of God that we will be changed into an eternal personality in an immortal body, and forever to be with the Lord Jesus Christ.

Chapter Nine

Rapture Pictures In Type

It is stated in Galatians 4:24, Colossians 4:17, and other scriptures that the holy days, Sabbath days, tabernacle, sacrifices, and personalities of the Old Testament were types or examples of things to come, even for the church. Certainly, the patriarchs and prophets were not informed about the coming Gentile church age; however, there could not be in revealed truth in the Old Testament anything that would contradict the eventual unveiling of the mystery of the dispensation of grace (Eph. 3:1-12). As Peter carefully stated regarding the conciliation of the two, *"And to this agree the words of the prophets. . . ."*

Not only was the translation of Enoch a type of the coming translation (Rapture) of the church, but there are also other types and allegories of this glorious event in the Old Testament. One of the more notable examples is the Song of Solomon.

Solomon married seven hundred wives and kept three hundred concubines. This particular biblical story was based upon one of the courtships of the king when he was still quite young. While there are different interpretations of the Song, it appears that Solomon owned a vineyard at Baal-Hamon in the territory of Asher in northern Israel. The vineyard was not producing because the keepers were not attending it, and the birds and wild animals were eating the grapes. So Solomon, disguised as a shepherd, went to Baal-Hamon to inspect his vineyard. While there, he met a beautiful girl of common birth, a Shulamite maiden. He fell in love with her and she returned his love. He had to return to Jerusalem on business, but before leaving he promised her he would return and make her his bride. Solomon kept his promise and carried her away to his palace, where they were married and became one. Although the new bride lived in splendor in the court, she longed for the beautiful hills and vineyards of Baal-Hamon, so Solomon went back with her for a visit.

As beautiful as the story is, the lesson is not in the literal account, but in the typeology. In the Song, Solomon becomes a type of the Lord Jesus Christ and the Shulamite maiden a type of the church. Only such an expressive love story could illustrate the love of the Lord Jesus for His Body of redeemed ones, His church: *"Husbands, love your wives, even as Christ also loved the church, and gave himself of it"* (Eph. 5:25).

We read in the tenth chapter of 1 Kings about the great wealth of Solomon, the richest king who ever lived to that time. In this, Solomon also represented the Lord Jesus Christ, the Creator of the Universe, Who came to earth as a poor man with no place to even lay His head. Solomon, the richest of men, went to Baal-Hamon disguised as a poor shepherd.

We read in Isaiah 5:7, *"For the vineyard of the Lord of hosts is the house of Israel. . . ."* And Jesus said in Matthew 15:24, *". . . I am not sent but unto the lost sheep of the house of Israel."* Likewise, Solomon went as a shepherd to his vineyard at Baal-Hamon. It appears from the wording in the Song that the keepers of the vineyard did not recognize Solomon and cast him out, just as Israel did not recognize Jesus Christ as the Messiah, the King of Glory. And as we read in John 1:11-12:

> *"He came unto his own, and his own received him not. But as many as received him, to them gave he power to become the sons of God, even to them that believe on his name."*

Even though Solomon was rejected by his own keepers at Baal-Hamon, there was one who did not reject him, a Shulamite maiden. Solomon in Hebrew means "peaceful" or interpreted, "prince of peace." Shulamite is the feminine form of Solomon, meaning "daughter of peace." The Shulamite addresses her shepherd friend in verse seven, chapter one of the Song:

> *"Tell me, O thou whom my soul loveth, where thou feedest, where thou makest thy flock to rest at noon. . . ."*

The response in type in the New Testament would be, *"I am the good shepherd, and know my sheep, and am known of mine. . . ."* (John 10:14). The relationship that developed between the two is illustrated in the Song 2:14 as Solomon speaks:

> *"O my dove, thou art in the clefts of the rock, in the secret places of the stairs, let me see thou countenance, let me hear thy voice; for sweet is thy voice, and thy countenance is comely."*

We may find it objectionable that Solmon married seven hundred wives and kept three hundred concubines. But in his life, Solomon was living out a type. His marriage to women out of every race and nation typified the coming of Jesus Christ to call out of every nation His church, or bride. We read in John 3:16 that *"God so loved the world . . ."* and that He is able to save to the uttermost all who believe in His only Son, Jesus Christ.

In the course of time, the relationship between Solomon and the maiden of Baal-Hamon reached the point where the Shulamite maiden introduced him to her family. We read in the Song 3:4:

> *". . . I found him whom my soul loveth: I held him, and would not let him go, until I had brought him into my mother's house. . . ."*

The mother of the Shulamite maiden is representative of the nations in which members of Christ's bride, the church, reside. The members of the bride of Jesus Christ, the church, are to introduce Him to the nations.

Solomon appears at the Shulamite's home as declared in the Song 2:9:

> *"My beloved is like a roe or a young hart: behold, he standeth behind our wall, he looketh forth at the windows, shewing himself through the lattice."*

The type here is fulfilled in Revelation 3:20:

> *"Behold, I stand at the door, and knock: if any man hear my voice, and open the door, I will come in to him, and will sup with him, and he with me."*

As the Shulamite opens the door to Solomon, we read his salutation in the next two verses:

*"My beloved spake, and said unto me, Rise up,
my love, my fair one, and come away. For, lo,
the winter is past, the rain is over and gone; The
flowers appear on the earth; the time of the
singing of birds is come, and the voice of the
turtle is heard in our land"* (Song 2:10-12).

It is here that Solomon suggests a marital relationship
as the Shulamite invites him through the door. The voice
of the turtle speaks of the Holy Spirit coming into the life
of a new Christian by faith. We read in Matthew 3:16 that
the dove is a symbol of the Holy Spirit, and Solomon
introduces a new life for her, one in which the birds are
singing and the flowers are blooming. The type again is
fulfilled in the words of Jesus in Luke 12:27-31:

*"Consider the lilies how they grow: they toil not,
they spin not; and yet I say unto you, that
Solomon in all his glory was not arrayed like
one of these. If then God so clothe the grass,
which is to day in the field, and to morrow is cast
into the oven; how much more will he clothe
you, O ye of little faith? And seek not ye what ye
shall eat, or what ye shall drink, neither be ye of
doubtful mind. For all these things do the
nations of the world seek after: and your Father
knoweth that ye have need of these things. But
rather seek ye the kingdom of God; and all these
things shall be added unto you."*

There are many other truths in the Song which
present in type the relationship between the church and
Jesus Christ. We read in the Song 4:12, *"A garden
inclosed is . . . my spouse; a spring shut up, a fountain*

sealed." The church is also a sanctified spouse as stated in 2 Corinthians 11:2:

> "For I am jealous over you with godly jealousy: for I have espoused you to one husband, that I may present you as a chaste virgin to Christ."

Like the Shulamite as an enclosed spring, the church is to be a pure well of water, springing up unto eternal life.

In verse one of chapter five we have a picture of the Passover supper that Jesus ate with His disciples:

> "I am come into my garden, my sister, my spouse: I have gathered my myrrh with my spice; I have eaten my honeycomb with my honey; I have drunk my wine with my milk: eat, O friends. . . ."

Myrrh and spices were not common for a dinner or Passover as they were used more often to put in the tomb with the body of the deceased. Also, Jesus addressed Judas as friend when He was betrayed in the Garden of Gethsamane. The Passover scene introduces a disturbing nightmare by the Shulamite:

> "I sleep, but my heart waketh: it is the voice of my beloved that knocketh, saying, Open to me, my sister, my love, my dove, my undefiled: for my head is filled with dew, and my locks with the drops of the night. I have put off my coat; how shall I put it on? I have washed my feet; how shall I defile them? My beloved put in his hand by the hole of the door, and my bowels were moved for him. I rose up to open to my

beloved; and my hands dropped with myrrh,
and my fingers with sweet smelling myrrh, upon
the handle of the lock" (Song 5:2-5).

In this nightmare, the Shulamite maiden sees Solomon standing at her door. His body is wet with sweat and his hair wet with dew, indicating a night scene, portraying the agony of Jesus when he prayed in Gethsemane and sweat drops of blood. His feet have been washed and anointed for burial, and his coat is on the ground, possibly referring to the soldiers casting lots for Jesus' coat while He was being crucified. The Shulamite maiden attempts to open the door and help her betrothed, but she has been handling myrrh and cannot grip the latch. Finally the Shulamite is able to open the latch:

"I opened to my beloved; but my beloved had
withdrawn himself, and was gone: my soul
failed when he spake: I sought him, but I could
not find him; I called him, but he gave me no
answer. The watchmen that went about the city
found me, they smote me, they wounded me, the
keepers of the walls took away my veil . . ."
(vss. 6-7).

This passage clearly identifies with the despair of the disciples after the crucifixion of Jesus and His ascension back to Heaven. But the people of Jerusalem asked the Shulamite maiden why, if she was so sad, didn't she just look for another lover. Her reply is given in verses ten through sixteen:

"My beloved is white and ruddy, the chiefest
among ten thousand. His head is the most fine

gold, his locks are bushy, and black as a raven. His eyes are as the eyes of doves by the rivers of waters, washed with milk, and fitly set. His cheeks are as a bed of spices, as sweet flowers: his lips like lilies, dropping sweet smelling myrrh. His hands are as gold rings set with the beryl: his belly is as bright ivory overlaid with sapphires. His legs are as pillars of marble set upon sockets of fine gold: his countenance is as Lebanon, excellent as the cedars, His mouth is most sweet: yea, he is altogether lovely. This is my beloved, and this is my friend, O daughters of Jerusalem."

The description of Solomon given by the Shulamite maiden corresponds with that of Jesus on the Mount of Transfiguration and that of the Apostle John in the first chapter of Revelation. The women of Jerusalem mocked the Shulamite maiden, asking her where her lover could have possibly gone, and she replied:

"My beloved is gone down into his garden, to the beds of spices, to feed in the gardens, and to gather lilies" (Song 6:2).

Jesus said to one of the thieves on the cross, *"Today shalt thou be with me in paradise."* Paradise means a beautiful park or garden, the place to which the Shulamite maiden said her betrothed had gone.

The Shulamite maiden awakens from her dream to find that Solomon has left his vineyard with the promise that he will return, and she takes care of it until he will come back for her. Then one days as she is working, she looks to the horizon and exclaims:

"Who is this that cometh out of the wilderness like pillars of smoke, perfumed with myrrh and frankincense, with all powders of the merchant? Behold his bed, which is Solomon's; threescore valiant men are about it, of the valiant of Israel. They all hold swords, being expert in war: every man hath his sword upon his thigh because of fear in the night" (Song 3:6-8).

The Shulamite maiden's betrothed is returning to her, not as the lowly shepherd when he came the first time, but as the mighty king surrounded by an army with drawn swords because the night is coming in which there is much danger. Solomon catches up his bride and sweeps her away, back to Jerusalem, where she reigns as queen. At the conclusion of the Song of Solomon, when she returns to Baal-Hamon with the king, she is so changed that no one recognizes her, as we read in the Song 8:5: *"Who is this that cometh up from the wilderness, leaning upon her beloved? . . ."*

The conclusion of the drama of Solomon and the Shulamite maiden presents in type the translation of the church as foretold in 1 Thessalonians 4:16-17:

"For the Lord himself shall descend from heaven with a shout, with the voice of the archangel, and with the trump of God: and the dead in Christ shall rise first: Then we which are alive and remain shall be caught up together with them in the clouds, to meet the Lord in the air: and so shall we ever be with the Lord."

The changing of the Shulamite maiden into a beautiful queen, adorned in gowns and jewels, illustrates the changing of our vile bodies into a glorious immortal body:

> *"Behold, I shew you a mystery; We shall not all sleep, but we shall all be changed, In a moment, in the twinkling of an eye, at the last trump: for the trumpet shall sound, and the dead shall be raised incorruptible, and we shall be changed"* (1 Cor. 15:51-52).

When Jesus Christ returns at the conclusion of the Tribulation period to save Israel, He will come as the Shulamite maiden saw Solomon returning, as King of kings with the armies of Heaven (Rev. 19:12-13).

In reference to those things which the Old Testament people experienced, Paul stated 1 Corinthians 10:11:

> *"Now all these things happened unto them for ensamples: and they are written for our admonition, upon whom the ends of the world are come."*

Like the example of Enoch and the story of the Song of Solomon, there are many types and illustrations in the Old Testament that hold the promise of Rapture and resurrection for Christians today.

Chapter Ten

Rapture Chronology

---

*"When they therefore were come together, they
asked of him, saying, Lord, wilt thou at this time
restore again the kingdom to Israel? And he said
unto them, It is not for you to know the times or
the seasons, which the Father hath put in his
own power"* (Acts 1:6-7).

This was a question which the apostles and disciples
asked Jesus all through His ministry from the time He
performed His first miracle at Cana until He died on the
cross. Never, at any time, did Jesus say He would never
restore the Kingdom to Israel. The promise of a Kingdom
in which Israel would be blessed above all nations and be
a witness for God to all people on earth is found in almost
every book of the prophets. If there is not to be such a
kingdom, then the Bible cannot be trusted as the Word of
God. Jesus taught the disciples to pray, *"Thy kingdom
come, thy will be done, on earth as it is in heaven."* Would
our Lord instruct His disciples to pray for an impossibility?
God's will has not been done on earth, neither is His
Kingdom come as yet on earth.

Jesus was hailed by the angels at His birth as heir to
the throne of David. Acts 15 clearly teaches that after the
church age, Jesus will return and restore the tabernacle

and the throne of David. Peter and John preached in Acts 3 that if Israel would repent of killing the Messiah, and cry out to God to send Him back, He would have come back at that time and brought in the Kingdom.

Revelation 20 clearly states that Jesus Christ will reign on this earth for a thousand years. This thousand years, according to Isaiah, Joel, Amos, Zechariah, and others, will be a time when there will be peace on earth; the nations will beat war implements into plowshares; crime and lawlessness will be restrained; ecology will be perfect; hunger will be no more, and there will be no unemployment. The end of the Kingdom age is not generally mentioned in the Old Testament. However, Joel, Isaiah, and a few of the prophets wrote about the astral catastrophe that will destroy this planet. We read in Isaiah 65:17:

"For, behold, I create new heavens and a new earth: and the former shall not be remembered, nor come into mind."

From Hebrews 4:1-8, and other scriptures, it is concluded that the Sabbath, the seventh day when God rested, was a type of the coming Kingdom age. With the biblical principle for time—one day as a thousand years—there is an indication that the Kingdom age would be a millennium, or one thousand years. However, such a conclusion is only that, but in Revelation 20 it is stated not once, but six times that this golden age will be one thousand years. In contemporary theology in regards to the roster of eschatological events, there are three main streams of thought in regard to the Kingdom age, or Millennium. They are . . .

Post-Millennialism

"Post" means after, or following. In respect to the return of Jesus Christ, this means that He will come after the Millennium, or at the end of a golden age of mankind brought about by the preaching of the gospel of all the earth. In other words, the church will bring in the Kingdom in which God's will would be done on earth, and then Jesus Christ will come back to reign and rule over the nations.

Post-millennialism probably arose with the development of Roman Catholicism, dating from the reign of Constantine. Post-millennialism theology could have been the impetus which motivated the spread of Catholicism to the new world. In 1700, post-millennialism took a new direction with the revisions of Daniel Whitby, and still later in the mid-nineteenth century, theistic evolutionists saw the upward progress of mankind continuing until the Millennium would appear. In the early twentieth century, many theologians saw socialism as an extension of the gospel, whereby hunger and war would be abolished and the promised Millennium would be realized. This is why many of the prominent theologians in the Federal Council of Churches, and later the World Council of Churches, were acknowledged socialists or communists.

Post-millennial theology thrived after World War One; however, World War Two, with the Nazi regime rising up in the heart of Protestantism, caused many ministers and proponents of this section of prophetic interpretation to come to the conclusion that the world was not getting better and better. Thus, post-millennialism has lost much of its following in many churches, denominations, and seminaries. Many who espoused this futuristic concept that the world is getting better became disillusioned.

There is a revival of sorts in pseudo-post-millennial theology today based on the New Age religion and the promises of a New World Order. These new heaven-on-earth ideas are invading an increasing number of liberal and modernistic churches.

A-Millennialism

"A" means no in Latin; therefore, the A-millennial teachings relating to eschatology means simply that there will be no Millennium—no one thousand years of Jesus Christ reigning on earth as stated in Revelation 20. The ages will continue in which the church carries out its mission while the history of man fluctuates between good and evil. When the earth has served its purpose, a time in the future which really cannot be determined, it will be destroyed and those saved at the single judgment of the dead will be resurrected and serve God forever.

In the late second century A.D., the seminary at Alexandria, Egypt, with the roots of its teaching grounded in Gnosticism, had practically subverted and changed most of the basic fundamentals of the faith, and its influence continued until the third and fourth centuries. In the late fourth century, there arose a defender of the Christian faith—Augustine, bishop of Hippo. Augustine had much influence in negating much of the destructive theology coming out of Egypt in regard to many basic Christian tenets; i.e., discipleship, service, salvation, authority of scripture, etc. However, the good bishop did not attend to defend the literal interpretation and application of the prophetic Word. After all, Jesus Christ had been dead almost five hundred years, there was no Jewish nation, and it did not appear there would ever be one again. Augustine proposed that the binding of Satan had occurred during the ministry of Jesus on earth, that the Millennium was already in progress, and that the church had assumed all the promises made to Israel in the Old Testament. Such an explanation relieved ministers of God from any major concern about the future as far as comparing prophecies with signs of the times, and this made for a very easy and comfortable position on eschatology. Or, as Peter wrote:

> *"Knowing this first, that there shall come in the last days scoffers, walking after their own lusts. And saying, Where is the promise of his coming? for since the fathers fell alseep, all things continue as they were from the beginning of the creation. For this they willingly are ignorant . . ."* (2 Pet. 3:3-5).

A-millennialism has prevailed as the dominant, doctrinal position on eschatology from the fifth century to the present. However, it has come under heavy attack in light of hard realism in the latter half of the twentieth century: wars and rumors of wars; pestilences like AIDS; a coming federated European empire; the rebirth of Israel and plans to resume Temple worship; computers making possible the mark of the Beast; increase of knowledge and communications; increase in earthquakes; a coming New World Order; nuclear missiles, etc. A-millennialists today are finding it increasingly difficult to defend their position on prophecy.

Pre-Millennialism

The prefix "pre" means before, or preceding; thus in

reference to eschatology, pre-millennialism means that Jesus Christ will return before the Millennium. In other words, as pre-millennialists interpret scripture, to destroy the armies of the nations and as stated in Revelation 11:18, ". . . *destroy them which destroy the earth.*"

It is obvious from the book of Acts and the epistles of Paul that the early Christians expected Jesus Christ to return in their lifetime. Even after A.D. 70, the church fathers looked forward to the return of Jesus to bring in the Kingdom upon earth as literally promised. In the early church of the first and second centuries, men like Justin Martyr, Barnabas, Melito, Tatian, Irenaeus, Tertullian, and a host of others were staunch pre-millennialists. Gibbons in *The Rise and Fall of the Roman Empire* wrote that the "reigning sentiment" of the early church was that Jesus Christ would return to bring in the Millennium in the year A.D. 2000, basing their belief on the seven days of the Genesis creation.

To present a complete study on pre-millennialism would require much more time and space than we could afford. Suffice it to say that most pre-millennialists today, in comparing the signs of the times with the prophetic Word, believe that we are living in the extremity of the church age and Jesus Christ could come at any time.

The Rapture Setting

The next item, in conjunction with the three divisions of eschatology relating to Christ's return to consider is the translation of the church, or Rapture, as presented in 1 Corinthians 15 and 1 Thessalonians 4. It is difficult for even A-millennialists and post-millennialists to spiritualize this resurrection promise. A-millennialists see the resurrection of Christians as a part of a general resurrection applying to all who ever lived—both the saved and unsaved. They do not see it as a unique circumstance relating only to the church of the dispensation of grace. Post-millennialists generally explain the resurrection of Christians as rising up to meet Jesus in the air, and then returning immediately with Him in glorified bodies, with no separate time span between rising to meet Him in the air and then returning to earth.

Pre-millennialists views as pertaining to the Rapture are more varied and complicated.

Partial Rapture

There are some, usually of Pentecostal persuasion, who teach that only the sanctified who are living overcoming lives, those who have spotless wedding garments, will be taken up to meet the Lord in the air. The rest will be left on earth to go through the Tribulation, or at least, part of it. Those who teach this view of the Rapture usually apply the parable of the ten virgins to substantiate this interpretation. However, it is difficult to find any scripture in reference to the church that supports a partial Rapture.

Paul addressed 1 Corinthians to a selfish, quarrelling, doctrinally confused, worldly church. Yet, he wrote to them in 1 Corinthians 15:51-52:

> *"Behold, I shew you a mystery; We shall not all sleep, but we shall **all** be changed, **In a moment, in the twinkling of an eye**. . . ."*

There is certainly no room here for a partial Rapture theory. Again, we read in 1 Thessalonians 4:13-18 where there is absolutely no indication of taking part of the

Christians at the Rapture and leaving the rest behind. Paul states over and over—we, we, we, we (no exception) shall be caught up to meet the Lord in the air. Of all the various Rapture positions, the partial Rapture is the weakest.

Post-Trib Rapture

While the post-Tribulaton position may be embraced by A-millennialists and post-millennialists alike, depending upon their own interpretations of the end of the age, it is also held by many pre-millennialists. While these pre-mil Christians believe that Jesus Christ is coming back to establish His Kingdom on earth for a thousand years, they also believe that the church will have to go through the Tribulation. The church is placed within the context of the Olivet Discourse in Matthew 24, whereas pre-Trib interpretations do not have the church in the Olivet Discourse.

An examination of Acts 15:14-17 helps to generally locate the time of the Rapture:

> *"Simeon hath declared how God at the first did visit the Gentiles, to take out of them a people for his name. And to this agree the words of the prophets; as it is written"* (vs. 14-15).

It is evident that the people who are being taken out of the Gentiles for the Name of God are those saved during this dispensation by the gospel of grace. This is the church.

> *"After this I will return, and will build again the tabernacle of David, which is fallen down; and I*

will build again the ruins thereof, and I will set it up" (vs. 16).

After God has finished calling out of the Gentiles a people for His Name, then Jesus will return (afterward) and rebuild the tabernacle of David. With the finishing of the church age, the calling out of the Gentiles, Jesus Christ will return literally to this earth to rebuild the tabernacle in accordance with the prophecy of Ezekiel, Isaiah, Amos, etc. This time of the church's completion is also called the "fulness of the Gentiles" (Rom. 11:25). The "calling out" will be completed at the Rapture, ending the church age, by any standard of interpration. Therefore, Jesus will not come back to put down all authority and rebellion and set up His Kingdom until "after" the church has been raptured. Both are not one unified or common event.

The coming of Jesus Christ projected in Matthew 24 is as ". . . *lightning cometh out of the east.*" This is not the way He will come for the church, and neither is Matthew 24:13 a message from the gospel of grace, ". . . *he that shall endure unto the end, the same shall be saved.*" More reasons why the church will not go through the Tribulation will be given in the discussion of pre-Tribulation Rapture.

Mid-Trib—Pre-Wrath Rapture

Another explanation of the Rapture on God's prophetic clock that has gained a following in recent years is the mid-Trib and/or pre-wrath Rapture. The mid-Trib position is that the church will go through the first three and a half years of the Tribulation period and then be raptured at the time when the Antichrist commits the Abomination of Desolation.

The assumption is that while there may be hard times during the first half, such as hunger, social unrest, revolutions, etc., there will be no major catastrophes or genocide until the second half. Those who teach mid-Trib Rapture generally believe that the Christians must be prepared to endure a time of persecution, but not wholesale extermination. Nevertheless, to conclude that the first half of the Tribulation is to be relatively free of massive extermination cannot be substantiated with scripture. In Revelation 6 at the conclusion of the opening of the fourth seal, one-fourth of the entire population of earth will have died from hunger, war, and related causes. That would mean over a billion people according to the present world population.

In Daniel 9 the prophet was given a time period of seventy weeks, beginning from a certain event, until the promises made by God to Israel would be fulfilled. These were weeks of years, or four hundred ninety years. Four hundred and sixty-three years transpired to the time of the cutting off (crucifixion) of the Messiah. The last week, or seven years, remains to be accounted for in the future. It is to begin with the Antichrist signing a general Middle East peace treaty, "confirming the covenant" with Israel, meaning granting Israel the right to the land that God gave the seed of Abraham through Isaac. In the middle of the week, after three and a half years (forty-two months), the Antichrist breaks the covenant and commits the Abomination of Desolation. If the church is to go through the first half of the Tribulation, then Christians will know the exact date the Rapture will occur.

The Abomination of Desolation is mentioned three times in Daniel, once by Jesus in Matthew 24, referred to by Paul in 2 Thessalonians 2:4, and by John in Revelation 13. In Matthew 24 Jesus mentions the Abomination of

Desolation as a sign to Israel that the last half of the Tribulation, the time of Jacob's Trouble, is at hand. Paul refers to the Abomination of Desolation in 2 Thessalonians 2 as a counter sign, to point out to Christians at Thessalonica that although they were suffering tribulation, that there was no way they could be in the Tribulation period foretold by Daniel and Jesus. Paul indicated that "that day" (day of the Lord, Tribulation) will not come except:

1. The falling away or departure, and then
2. The "man of sin be revealed."

When will the man of sin be revealed? When he signs the covenant with Israel. Paul did not say that Christians would be on earth to witness the Abomination of Desolation. He gave it only as a sign that the Christians at Thessalonica were **not** in the day of the Lord.

Those who believe in the mid-Trib Rapture, or pre-wrath Rapture, cite the "last trump" of 1 Corinthians 15:52 as the last trumpet of Revelation, to try to prove that the Rapture occurs during the middle or last part of the Tribulation. In reading scriptures in the Bible in reference to the blowing of trumpets, trumpets were usually blown to signal assembly, victory, feast days, and less often to signal a warning of the approach of enemies or danger. The seven trumpets of Revelation are heralders of judgment. The trumpet of 1 Corinthians 15:52, therefore, cannot be the last trump of Revelation.

As far as the pre-wrath Rapture teaching is concerned, God indeed does preserve His own from His wrath of judgment. God saving Noah through the flood is one example; the saving of Lot and his family from Sodom is another. And there is no doubt but that the seventh trumpet of Revelation announces judgments upon earth in accordance with the wrath of God. However, from the entire scope of the Tribulation in Revelation, from chapters six through nineteen, the wrath of God is declared. We read in Revelation 6:17, *"For the great day of his wrath is come and who shall be able to stand?"* With the blowing of the first trumpet, all grass is burned and a third part of the trees. At the blowing of the second trumpet one-third of the ships will be destroyed and the sea will become as blood. When the third trumpet is sounded, many men die. At the sounding of the sixth trumpet, a third of all left alive will be killed. This is not wrath? In the light of the entire scope of Tribulation judgments, the mid-Trib and pre-wrath Rapture positions seem to fall apart.

Pre-Trib Rapture

According to our Lord Jesus Christ, a time of trouble, such as the world has never seen before, will precede His return. According to Revelation 13:5; 12:14, and Daniel 9:27, we know this time of Great Tribulation, in which there will be mass starvation, mass destruction, and religious persecution, will last for seven years. We believe the Rapture of the church occurs at the beginning of the Tribulation. Therefore, we submit ten scriptural reasons why we accept a pre-Trib Rapture:

1. Jesus Christ will come at the beginning of the Tribulation to Rapture the church. He will return to the earth at the end of the Tribulation to destroy the Antichrist and his armies, save a remnant of Israel, and bring in His Kingdom from Heaven upon the earth. Paul said that Jesus would come in

the air for the church, but when He returns at the end of the Tribulation to Israel, His feet will stand upon the Mount of Olives and He will reign on David's throne (Zech. 14:4).

2. The Tribulation period is always spoken of in the Bible as the night in which the Lord will return as a thief. The Tribulation period is also the beginning of the day of the Lord. After Paul had finished the description of the Rapture at the end of the fourth chapter of 1 Thessalonians, he continued on the same subject in chapter five:

"But of the times and the seasons, brethren, ye have no need that I write unto you. For yourselves know perfectly that the day of the Lord so cometh as a thief in the night. For when they [the unsaved] *shall say, Peace and safety; then sudden destruction cometh upon them* [not Christians], *as travail upon a woman with child; and they shall not escape. But ye, brethren, are not in darkness, that that day should overtake you as a thief"* (1 Thess. 5:1-4).

Nothing is said here by Paul about Christians being in the night, in the day of the Lord, or this time of great destruction. Every indication is that the unsaved will be in the Tribulation, but Christians will not have to fear this terrible night, because we are of the day.

3. Every scripture dealing with the Rapture of the church indicates that only Christians will see Jesus at this glorious event. They will not see Him until they rise up into the air and meet Him. The translation of the church will be like the translation

of Enoch. No one will know what has suddenly happened to cause the disappearance of millions of people. However, every scripture mentioning the literal return of Jesus Christ as King of kings at the end of the Tribulation indicates that every person in the world will see Him (Matt. 24:30; Rev. 1:7).

4. Those living during the Tribulation will be warned by God not to take the mark of the Beast or they will be eternally lost in Hell. No such warning is given to the church in the Pauline epistles. If the church is to go through the Tribulation, then Paul would have forewarned Christians living in the last days about the mark of the Beast. Instead, Paul wrote in Ephesians 1:13-14 that the salvation of Christians is sealed by the Holy Spirit until the day of redemption.

5. It is generally agreed that the seven churches of Revelation represent the churches down through the dispensation of grace. It is evident that the Tribulation period begins in the fifth chapter of Revelation, and ends with the twentieth chapter. We find eighteen references to church or churches in the first three chapters of Revelation, but not a single reference to a church, or churches, from chapter four through chapter twenty. The logical conclusion is that there will be no Christian church in the world during the Tribulation.

6. Scriptures relating to the coming of the Lord to reign on the earth, that is, when He comes all the way to the earth at the end of the Tribulation, refer to Him as the Son of man. But Jesus is never addressed by the church, which is bound for heavenly places, as the Son of man. In the epistles

to the church, Jesus is called the Son of God. Speaking of His literal return to the earth, Jesus said in Matthew 24:30:

". . . all the tribes of the earth mourn, and they shall see the Son of man coming in the clouds of heaven with power and great glory."

In no scripture referring to the Rapture and translation of the church is Jesus referred to as the Son of man. If the church were to go through the Tribulation, the Christians also would be admonished to look for the Son of man coming as King of kings.

7. The Holy Spirit is the Restrainer of lawlessness in the world, because He reproves the world of sin. The Holy Spirit also ministers through Christians to reprove the world of sin. But 2 Thessalonians 2:7-12 indicates that the Holy Spirit will be taken out of the way so that a state of lawlessness will prevail over the world to make way for the man of sin—the Antichrist. Paul wrote that this must happen so that the time of great wickedness called the Tribulation period can be brought in. Inasmuch as the Holy Spirit will be taken out of the way, it is evident that the Christians will also be removed from the world.

8. The Christians at Thessalonica were confused about the Great Tribulation. They were undergoing such persecution they believed they were already in this terrible period of time. And so Paul wrote to them about the Rapture. In 2 Thessalonians 2:1 the apostle called the Rapture *". . . our gathering together unto him."* However, he separated the

Rapture, or the gathering of the church to the Lord, and His coming all the way to the earth. Paul then referred to some events of the Tribulation that the Christians at Thessalonica would know of a certainty that they were not in the Tribulation, and nowhere within the context of Paul's second epistle to the church at Thessalonica does he place the church within the Tribulation. In fact, in the first chapter Paul said that Christ was coming back in great power with fire to punish them on the earth, taking vengeance. The remnant of Israel to be saved will be in a special place, which many believe to be Petra. If the church is left on earth, then Christians will suffer the vengeance of the Lord, which is unthinkable.

9. The Great Tribulation, the time of Jacob's Trouble, is to prepare a remnant of Israel to receive the Lord Jesus Christ as their Messiah when He comes. Christians are already a prepared people for a prepared place. There is no reason to leave the church in the Tribulation.

10. The signs given to the church of the last days are: a falling away from the faith, many following after seducing spirits; the breakup of the home; juvenile delinquency; liars and deceivers. Nowhere does Paul give the church the signs mentioned in the heavens, terrible heat and the plagues mentioned that would come during the Tribulation. God translated Enoch before the judgment of the flood, and He made a way of escape for Noah. Enoch is a type of the church, and Noah a type of faithful Israel. God also called Lot out of Sodom before judgment fell. It is

also evident that He will call the church out of the
world before the judgment of the Tribulation falls.

Chapter Eleven

Resurrection Activity
In the Tribulation

The Revelation begins with the word *apokalupsis*, meaning to reveal, uncover, or expose. Jesus Christ is the Exposer, and John is the exposee, so in turn you and I are included as exposees. The problem is to know just to what we are being exposed.

Also in verse one we are informed that the things being revealed to John are to *tachos* (quickly, speedily) come to pass. This could be interpreted, and has been interpreted, to mean that the events revealed to John are to transpire quickly, in rapid succession, meaning that the entire scope of the "apocalypse" is a relatively brief time.

Next, we note in verse three that God's blessing is upon those who read this prophecy, with the qualification that they keep the things they read in this book. Now then, does Jesus mean that we are to not worship the Beast, keep from taking his mark, and endure until the end of the apocalypse? It is obvious that today, you and I cannot keep the things written in this book, unless we take the position of the Seventh Day Adventists that worshipping on Sunday is the mark of the Beast, and the entire Revelation is to be interpreted historically, which makes absolutely no sense at all.

Next, we notice at the conclusion of verse three, *". . . the time is at hand."* What is at hand? Evidently it is the event mentioned in verse seven of chapter one:

"Behold, he cometh with clouds; and every eye shall see him, and they also which pierced him. . . ."

Therefore, it would seem evident that everything in Revelation is to happen immediately before the coming of Jesus Christ to assume His position as the "prince of the kings of the earth." Certainly, Jesus Christ is not the prince of the kings of the earth today.

In verse four John stated, or at least indicated, the apocalypse was for the seven churches in Asia, specifically named in verse eleven. In verse ten we read, *"I was in the Spirit on the Lord's day. . . ."* The common interpretation of this statement is that John was filled with the Holy Spirit as he was worshipping on Sunday. While the early church fathers like Barnabas, Polycarp, Justin Martyr, Tertullian, and others, did recognize Sunday as the honorable day of assembly and worship of the Lord, Sunday is never called the Lord's day in the Bible. The Lord's day in scripture always means the Tribulation period, so John's statement could just as well be interpreted to mean that he was transported by the Holy Spirit into the Tribulation, where he saw the things revealed to him by Jesus Christ.

John was on the Isle of Patmos, a political prisoner of the Roman Empire. I have been to Patmos several times and even visited the cave where John supposedly received the apocalypse.

In speaking to the seven churches of Asia, the apostle identifies himself also as their "companion in tribulation."

Inasmuch as John was a prisoner of Rome, in tribulation, in the Spirit on the day of the Lord, we may wonder if he is not a type of believers during the Tribulation period who will be under great tribulation from the Revived Roman Empire. The vision of Jesus Christ in chapter one is as coming Judge of the nations, King of kings, found only in one other place in the New Testament, the Mount of Transfiguration.

The messages to the seven churches of Asia are a mystery, and I have never heard or read any explanation that completely satisfied. Were there churches in these seven cities in A.D. 96? Possible, or even probable. We know there were churches at Ephesus and Laodicea. Were these seven letters actually sent by John to be read or distributed to these seven congregations? Possibly, but the language is foreign to the Gospel of grace. Certainly, even the most fundamental, evangelical church of today would have great trouble with the terminology. Could the churches, as many interpret, represent seven church ages from the first century to the return of Christ? Possibly, as there are similarities. Could these churches represent churches that will be in evidence at the end of the church age? Again, quite possible as we can identify these churches, in their merits and demerits, with types of churches today. Could these churches be literal churches, or representative of types of churches, that will be in the world during the Tribulation? This also is a possibility. I know of no churches in these cities today in Turkey, as that nation is predominantly Moslem. It is indeed possible that congregations of liberal churches, many of whom are unsaved, may be cast into the Tribulation. If all churches are cast into the Tribulation, then there is no pre-Trib Rapture, and Christians saved by the Gospel of grace will be under another Gospel whereby they could lose their salvation, which is unthinkable. Regardless of the difficult terminology with phrases like "enduring to the end," "a crown of life to those who overcome," and like promises and warnings, the real meaning of the seven letters is captured in the message to the church at Philadelphia, the church of brotherly love:

> *"Because thou hast kept the word of my patience, I also will keep thee from the hour of temptation, which shall come upon all the world, to try them that dwell upon the earth. Behold, I come quickly: hold that fast which thou hast, that no man take thy crown"* (Rev. 3:10-11).

This letter indicates that the Tribulation will come upon them that dwell in the world, the unsaved, but those who have been born again through faith in Jesus Christ will be kept from the Tribulation. However, due to godless conditions in the world, Christians are to be careful to remain steadfast in the faith lest they lose their rewards.

Now then, after Jesus Christ finished dictating seven letters to the seven letters, John writes:

> *"After this I looked, and, behold, a door was opened in heaven: and the first voice which I heard was as it were of a trumpet talking with me; which said, Come up hither, and I will shew thee things which must be hereafter"* (Rev. 4:1).

An accepted pre-Tribulation understanding of the Rapture is that after the church age ends, or as the church age ends, the Rapture will occur and then the Tribulation will begin. The eschatology of Revelation four through twenty-two has a setting from the translation of the church forward. And, from that point forward, Revelation 4:1, there is nothing to be joyful about concerning the status of people living on earth, until the events of Revelation unfold. In other words, from a worldly viewpoint, everything is negative from Revelation 4 to Revelation 20. The following chronology of Rapture and resurrection activity in Revelation after chapter four is as follows:

Souls Under the Altar

"And when he had opened the fifth seal, I saw under the altar the souls of them that were slain for the word of God, and for the testimony which they held: And they cried with a loud voice, saying, How long, O Lord, holy and true, dost thou not judge and avenge our blood on them that dwell on the earth? And white robes were given unto every one of them; and it was said unto them, that they should rest for a little season, until their fellowservants also and their brethren, that should be killed as they were, should be fulfilled" (Rev. 6:9-11).

Under the levitical law, as explained in Leviticus 4, blood from the sin offering was poured out on the bottom of the Altar of Burnt Offering. Jesus Christ referred to the martyrs of the Old Testament in Matthew 23:35:

". . . upon you [the religious leaders of Israel] *may come all the righteous blood shed upon the earth, from the blood of righteous Abel unto the blood of Zacharias son of Barachias, whom ye slew between the temple and the altar."*

This particular group of souls under the altar doubtless were those in the Old Testament who were called to die for their faith. Although Jesus Christ took the Paradise compartment of Hades with Him to Heaven, these Old Testament heroes of faith evidently did not enter God's presence. So they will be given white robes in the Tribulation, that is counted righteous, so that they might stand before the throne of God to bear witness of the justice of God as Tribulation judgments begin. They are also told to wait for a little season (probably the Tribulation period) until those who would be also killed for their faith in this "little season." Nothing is said here of the thousands of Christians martyred during the church age, because it appears evident that these martyrs have already received their glorified bodies at the Rapture.

Tribulation Martyrs

In the first eight verses of Revelation 7 is the account of one hundred forty-four thousand Israelites, twelve thousand from each of the twelve tribes of Israel, who will be sealed by God in their foreheads. The Antichrist will later attempt to seal his faithful followers in their foreheads with their own mark. The seal of God on the one hundred forty-four thousand Israelites is to protect them from being hurt by the judgments to come during the Tribulation. This is evident from the context.

The only Israelite tribal identification possible today is by name derivation—the Cohens (descendants of Aaron) and Jews with Levi in their family name. These are descendants of the priests and Levites. However, we can be sure that God knows the tribal connection of every Israelite; or, it may be possible that old family records dating to the time of the destruction of the Temple may be found. The theory that the ten tribes of the northern kingdom were all lost and showed up again as England, Denmark, the United States, etc., is completely without any basis of fact. Even after the Assyrian invasion and genocide against Israel in about 700 B.C., we read in the Bible that Israelites from all twelve tribes came to Jerusalem to observe the Passover.

Next, we read that following the sealing of the one hundred forty-four thousand, a great multitude coming out of all nations appeared before the throne of God in white robes. John adds that the number is so great that no man can count them, meaning that this congregation must figure into the millions, hundreds of millions, or even billions. In chapter six, the Old Testament martyrs are told to wait for justice until they are joined by those who will yet be martyred. Evidently, the multitudes in chapter seven appearing in white robes are the completed number of Tribulation martyrs, because we read in verse fourteen of chapter seven:

> *". . . These are they which came out of great tribulation, and have washed their robes, and made them white in the blood of the Lamb."*

Like the Old Testament martyrs, they appear in robes of righteousness in order to be in the presence of God, because they have not as yet received a resurrection body.

The basis of the salvation of this great multitude out of all nations is given in Revelation 12:11:

> *"And they overcame him by the blood of the Lamb, and by the word of their testimony; and they loved not their lives unto the death."*

In Revelation 13, John foretold that during the Tribulation, the Antichrist will command that every person in the world take his mark or number and worship him as God, or they will be killed. In Matthew 24:21, Jesus said:

"For then shall be great tribulation, such as was not since the beginning of the world to this time, no, nor ever shall be."

But of that day Jesus also said in verse thirteen, *"But he that shall endure unto the end, the same shall be saved."*

Overcoming and enduring during the Great Tribulation also includes refusing to take the mark of the Beast or to worship the Antichrist (Rev. 14:9-10). The scene John saw around the throne of God with all the Tribulation martyrs gathered illustrates the millions during the Great Tribulation who will be beheaded for not taking the mark of the Beast. It is commonly concluded by many who write commentaries on Revelation that this great multitude have been saved through the preaching of the one hundred forty-four thousand, but this is not what the scripture states. They may or may not have been ministered to by those Jewish witnesses or evangelists. The only thing we do know for sure is that they were saved by faith in Jesus Christ, and because of their faith in Jesus Christ as Savior and Lord, they refused to take the mark of the Beast because it would mean they would accept Satan's false christ as their God.

The resurrection of the Great Tribulation martyrs does not occur until Jesus Christ returns at the end of the Great Tribulation. Paul said that in the first resurrection— the resurrection of the saved—every man would be raised in his own particular order. Therefore, it seems evident that all martyrs of the Old Testament and those of the Tribulation period will constitute one particular order as declared in Revelation 20:4

> *"And I saw thrones, and they that sat upon them, and judgment was given unto them: and I saw the souls of them that were beheaded for the witness of Jesus, and for the word of God, and which had not worshipped the beast, neither his image, neither had received his mark upon their foreheads, or in their hands; and they lived and reigned with Christ a thousand years."*

According to Revelation 7, the Old Testament martyrs and the Great Tribulation martyrs will serve with Jesus Christ in the Millennial Temple. That will be a glorious reward, ministering day and night in the Millennial Temple for the Lord.

The size and description of the Millennial Temple are given in Ezekiel 40 through 47.

The One Hundred Forty-Four Thousand

Much ado is made about the one hundred forty-four thousand sealed Israelites, but we actually are not told very much about their mission. That they go into all the world and preach the gospel of the Kingdom during the Tribulation is a conclusion, although it may well be true. God has always had His witness in the world, regardless of the depth of human depravity. It appears the one hundred forty-four thousand begin their mission, regardless of its nature, a few days or weeks at most after the

Antichrist signs a covenant with Israel, which also could be construed to mean a general Middle East peace treaty. How long the one hundred forty-four thousand continue on their mission during the Tribulation is uncertain. Nothing is indicated about their being on earth when Christ returns at the end of the Tribulation. It seems apparent they will not be harmed by natural catastrophes, but nothing is said about protection against persecution by the Antichrist.

As indicated in 2 Thessalonians 2, the church and the Holy Spirit will be taken out of the way to allow the spirit of iniquity to come in to the fullest, and the same may be true of the one hundred forty-four thousand.

In Revelation 12 the symbolic teaching projects that after the Abomination of Desolation, Satan moves to completely destroy Israel, and in accordance with Jesus' warning in Matthew 24:15-21, the Jews escape to a place of safety where they hide for three and a half years until the Messiah—Jesus Christ—comes. After the Jews in Judea flee into the wilderness, which I believe to be Petra, we read in Revelation 12:17:

> *"And the dragon was wroth with the woman, and went to make war with the remnant of her seed, which keep the commandments of God, and have the testimony of Jesus Christ."*

The only Jews left who keep the commandments of God and have the testimony, or gospel, of Jesus Christ, will be the one hundred forty-four thousand. After the Antichrist is unsuccessful in surprising the Jews with a sudden attack, he turns on the one hundred forty-four thousand to kill them. In Revelation 13 he declares to all the world that every human being on planet earth must take his mark and worship him as God or be killed. And continuing immediately into chapter fourteen, we find the one hundred forty-four thousand singing a new song before the throne of God and being declared to be firstfruits unto God. It seems beyond question that "firstfruits" refers to the firstfruits of resurrection. Nothing is said about their having robes, as they appear without fault before the throne of God.

The most logical course of scripture concerning the one hundred forty-four thousand suggests that they are translated, or raptured, soon after the Abomination of Desolation is committed. They will not be part of the church and their translation will be an entirely separate event in the order of the first resurrection.

The Two Witnesses

Their Death and Resurrection

One of the most interesting, yet perplexing, incidents relating to resurrection and Rapture activity during the Tribulation is the ministry of the two witnesses of Revelation 11. The Apostle John sees the Temple of God, including the Altar of Burnt Offering, standing in Jerusalem, apparently on Mount Moriah. He also was given a measuring rod to see if it did indeed measure according to God's specifications. John was also to measure those who worshipped in the Temple, evidently to see if they also measured up to God's standards for true worshippers of Himself. The outer court was not to be measured, as it was designated as a place for Gentile tourism or worship.

Jesus prophesied that Jerusalem would be trodden down of the Gentiles until the "times of the Gentiles" be fulfilled (Luke 21:24). In 1967, Israel did retake the old part of Jerusalem, including the Temple Mount, but it is still designated as Israeli-occupied territory. The old city is still, for the most part, occupied by Arabs and Arab guards patrol the Temple Mount. John also is informed that Gentiles will be allowed in the court of the Temple, and that Jerusalem will be trodden down by them for forty-two months. Next, the angel informs John that God will give unusual powers to two witnesses, and their ministry will last for 1,263 days.

There is much speculation and conjecture as to whether the ministry of these two witnesses will occur during the first forty-two months of the Tribulation or the last forty-two months. It seems that their ministry will be extended three days beyond forty-two months, possibly allowing for the three days their bodies will lie in the streets of Jerusalem. Dr. John F. Walvoord favors the position that their ministry will be in the last half of the Tribulation due to the statement that Jerusalem will be trodden down by Gentiles during their ministry. It would appear from scripture that the Jews will be given control of the city and the Temple Mount so that the Temple can be rebuilt and sacrificial worship restored. The Antichrist steps in to take control of Jerusalem and commits the Abomination of Desolation at the Temple, and then the city will be completely under his authority the latter half of the Tribulation.

According to the description given of the power and ministry of the two witnesses, if anyone should be successful in hurting either one of the two witnesses, fire will come out of their mouths and incinerate that person. They will also have power to turn water into blood and bring all the plagues down upon the kingdom of Antichrist that Moses, by the power of God, brought upon Egypt. We notice also that they will hold back the rain for forty-two months, the approximate length of time that rain was withheld from Israel during the time of Elijah's ministry. The prophet Joel was given a vision of the latter half of the Tribulation when rain would be withheld, the grass and trees are burned, and the rivers no longer have water:

> *"Alas for the day! for the day of the Lord is at hand, and as a destruction from the Almighty it shall it come. Is not the meat cut off before our eyes, yea, joy and gladness from the house of our God? The seed is rotten under their clods, the garners are laid desolate, the barns are broken down; for the corn is withered. How do the beasts groan! the herds of cattle are perplexed, because they have no pasture; yea, the flocks of sheep are made desolate. O Lord, to thee will I cry: for the fire hath devoured the pastures of the wilderness, and the flame hath burned all the trees of the field. The beasts of the field cry also unto thee: for the rivers of water are dried up, and the fire hath devoured the pastures of the wilderness"* (Joel 1:15-20).

The day of the Lord is the Tribulation. Joy will be cut off from the Temple when the Antichrist stops the daily sacrifice and commits the Abomination of Desolation. From that time it will not rain for three and a half years, and all over the world the grass will be burned. Never, in the history of the world, has such a catastrophe occurred, but the Bible says that one day it will.

After the two supernatural witnesses have completed

the mission which the Lord will assign them, the Beast will kill them, and their bodies will lie in the street of the great city, spiritually called Sodom and Egypt, where Jesus was crucified. Of course, this could be no other city but Jerusalem. Egypt is synonymous with worldiness and Sodom with sinful abominations, a general description of the spiritual estate of Jerusalem under the administration of Antichrist.

When the time came for Jesus to be crucified, He said as recorded in Luke 13:33:

"Nevertheless I must walk to day, and to morrow, and the day following: for it cannot be that a prophet perish out of Jerusalem."

So a prophet had to be killed in Jerusalem, and Jesus hurried to Jerusalem to be killed and fulfill His mission of dying for the sins of the world. The two witnesses also must be prophets, and the two most likely candidates are Moses and Elijah. The plagues that Moses brought upon Egypt will be brought on the kingdom, and Elijah brought a great drought upon the nation of Israel during the reign of Jezebel and Ahab. The relationship of the Antichrist and the great religious whore of Revelation 17 also typifies the relationship that Ahab had with Jezebel.

One primary reason for the belief that Elijah will be one of the two witnesses is found in the third chapter of Malachi. The chapter begins by heralding a messenger who will prepare the way for the Lord to come to His Temple. Malachi also describes the results of the Lord's coming, prophecies that were not fulfilled at the first coming of Jesus. The chapter concludes with the promise:

"Behold, I will send you Elijah the prophet

*before the coming of the great and dreadful day
of the Lord"* (Mal. 4:5).

John the Baptist did come in the spirit of Elijah. His
clothes were like Elijah wore; his food was the same; and
his ministry was similar. Like Elijah stood before Ahab
and condemned his idolatrous relationship with Jezebel,
John stood before Herod and condemned his adulterous
relationship with his brother's wife, Herodias. It was
necessary for Jesus to have a forerunner like John the
Baptist in order to fulfill every Old Testament prophecy
identifying Him as the Messiah.

The reason I personally favor the identity of the two
witnesses as Moses and Elijah is that when Jesus on the
Mount of Transfiguration revealed to Peter, John, and
James His appearance as it would be when He came
again, Moses and Elijah appeared with Him. Then when
the three asked Jesus why the scribes said that Elijah must
come before the Kingdom and the Messiah appears, Jesus
replied, *"Elias truly shall first come, and restore all
things."* The Jews, in expectation of Elijah coming before
the Messiah, reserve a chair for him at the Passover table.

While it is true that Moses did die, Michael and the
Devil argued over his body. Also, Enoch was a prophet
because we read in Jude 14 that he prophesied about the
Lord's coming with His saints. Nevertheless, the entire
body of scripture relating to the ministry of the two
witnesses seems to favor Moses and Elijah. However, it is
entirely possible that the two witnesses will be neither
Moses nor Elijah, and Elijah's coming will be before their
mission.

Regardless of the identity of the two witnesses, after
their ministry is finished the Antichrist will kill them.
Their dead bodies will lie in the streets of Jerusalem for

three days. Jewish traditions stipulate that the body being lifeless for three days signifies total and irreversible death. During these three days all the world will view their bodies, now made possible by worldwide television networks. This event may occur at the Christmas season, as there will be great rejoicing over the victory of Antichrist over the two witnesses, and throughout the world people will send gifts to each other. Then, we read, as the world is rejoicing and watching, the bodies of the two witnesses come alive and they are raptured before the eyes of all the people on the earth. They are caught up in a cloud and rise up into the air, out of sight. The scripture states that they will ascend into Heaven in a cloud, and it is interesting that on the Mount of Transfiguration, Moses and Elijah descended in a cloud. What kind of a cloud this will be, we are not told. Paul does say that at the Rapture of the church, Christians will be caught up in clouds.

As the two witnesses rise in the air, a great earthquake shakes Jerusalem. One-tenth of the buildings in the city fall and seven thousand men will be killed. Then, a remnant of the Jews give glory to God. This could account for the act of Antichrist to stop worship at the Holy Place, and this remnant could be the Jews who then flee to Petra to be hid for three and a half years until Jesus returns.

The conclusion of the entire scope of death, Rapture, and resurrection during the Tribulation is the destruction of the armies of Antichrist and his consignment, along with the False Prophet, to the lake of fire. As far as can be determined from scripture, these two are the only ones who will be cast alive into the "lake of fire."

The Son of Perdition

There is a change in the verb tense in references to the

coming Antichrist in the Old Testament as we get into the New Testament. The Old Testament prophecies indicate the coming of the "wicked one" to be future, whereas, in the New Testament, he is presented as already being in existence.

Warnings are given in the prophecies from the Old Testament for Israel not to be foolish and accept a false prince as their Messiah in the last days. For example, we note the words of the prophet in Ezekiel 21:25-27:

> *"And thou, profane wicked prince of Israel, whose day is come, when iniquity shall have an end, Thus saith the Lord God; Remove the diadem, and take off the crown: this shall not be the same: exalt him that is low, and abase him that is high. I will overturn, overturn, overturn, it: and it shall be no more, until he come whose right it is; and I will give it him."*

The identity of the Antichrist as that "wicked one" is common in both the Old Testament and the New Testament. He is also called a prince of Israel, which indicates that he will be at least partly Jewish. He will not only be wicked, he will be profane, rejecting the "God of the fathers" (Dan. 11:37), and his speech will be filled with continual blasphemies against all that is holy and sacred (Rev. 13:6).

In speaking of the Antichrist in 2 Thessalonians 2:3, Paul calls him "that man of sin," not just "a" man of sin. This reference immediately identifies the Antichrist as a particular person. The apostle also speaks of his "revealing" as "the son of perdition," and not just "a" son of perdition. A thing or person cannot be revealed unless such an entity is already in existence—for example, the revealing or unveiling of a painting.

Jesus Christ is seated at the right hand of the Father until the time for His revealing to the world as King of kings and Lord of lords (Rev. 19). Likewise, the selection of definite articles used by Paul when speaking of the revealing of the "man of sin" as Antichrist signifies that the wicked one was in existence in a state of perdition at the time Paul wrote to the church at Thessalonica. This conclusion is verified by the very definition of the word perdition, which is interpreted thus in the *Critical Lexicon and Concordance*:

> *"Loss, destruction, ruin; the end pronounced upon all who, having heard the summons to repentance and faith in Christ, have persisted in impenitence. The loss of all that such ever had, or might have had for ever; the destruction of such, in body, soul, spirit, and utter and final ruin, which will not be reversed."*

It is understood that all who reject the salvation of God offered through the Lord Jesus Christ Who died for sin will go into perdition—an irreversible state of eternal shame and torment. However, the Bible speaks of "the son of perdition" in the same sense as it speaks of "**the** Son of God." We know there are many "sons of God." Adam is called "a son of God" because he was a direct creation of God (Luke 3:38). The angels are also called "sons of God" because they too are direct creations of the Creator (Gen. 6:2). Christians are "sons of God" by adoption through faith in Jesus Christ (Rom. 8:15-16). But, there is only one "**the** only begotten Son of God." According to the same scriptural rule, there are many sons of perdition, but there is only one individual who is "**the** son of perdition."

In considering clues to the possible identity of Antichrist, keep in mind that this wicked person will be in the world when Christ comes the second time. When the Lord returns, He will fulfill all the promises that are associated with His glorious reign given in the Old Testament. He will heal the sick, banish war, restore nature to perfection, enforce peace, and rule the nations with a rod of iron. But all the promises concerning the Messiah were fulfilled in type at His first coming. He opened the eyes of the blind, opened the ears of the deaf, made the lame to leap as a deer, etc. All these things He did so that the prophecies might be fulfilled and Israel be without excuse. It is noted in Zechariah 14:4 that at the time the Lord will be King over all the earth, He will stand upon Mount Olivet, and the mountain will split. When the time came for Jesus to present His claim to the throne of David, He departed from the Temple and went to Mount Olivet, but instead of standing—the biblical symbol for taking possession—He sat down. This gesture indicated that Jesus knew that He would be rejected; nevertheless, the promise was fulfilled in type.

The last prophecy recorded in the Old Testament is given in Malachi 4:5:

"Behold, I will send you Elijah the prophet before the coming of the great and dreadful day of the Lord."

When Jesus was asked the question where Elijah was, if He was indeed the Messiah, He pointed to John the Baptist, and answered that John would be Elijah if Israel would receive Him as Lord and King. And inasmuch as every prophecy concerning the appearance of the Messiah was fulfilled in part during the earthly ministry of Jesus, it is obvious that the wicked prince who would betray the Son of David and try to steal His throne must have also been present, at least in type, at the time. It seems apparent that the man who perfectly fits the prophetic type was Judas Iscariot.

In light of the definition of perdition, as pertaining to a state of utter ruin and damnation without end, let us think for a moment concerning the possible identity of "**the** son of perdition." The greatest prophetic identifying clue to the identity of Antichrist is that he will deny that Jesus Christ has already come in the flesh, and make the vast majority of the world believe the lie. And, if we were to consider every man and every woman who ever lived from Adam and Eve to this present time, who had the greatest opportunity to come to know Jesus Christ as both Lord and Savior, and yet turned away and not only rejected so great salvation, but denied Him as God's Son come in the flesh, that person would have to be Judas Iscariot. Judas, without question, would have to head the all-time list of all people who could have known without reservation that Jesus was the Christ, yet turned away and denied Him. Judas walked with Jesus for three and a half years; he witnessed the miracles of Jesus; he heard the messages of Jesus and the multitudes say, "no man ever spake like this man." Yet Judas never once considered receiving Jesus Christ as the Messiah. Jesus said of this lost disciple in John 17:12:

> *"While I was with them in the world, I kept them in thy name: those that thou gavest me I have kept, and none of them is lost, but **the son of perdition**. . . ."*

It is evident that Judas was in an irreversible state of

eternal damnation, even when he was numbered among the twelve.

Jesus called Judas "the son of perdition," and Paul wrote of the Antichrist in 2 Thessalonians 2:3-4:

> *"Let no man deceive you by any means: for that day shall not come, except there come a falling away first, and that man of sin be revealed, **the son of perdition**; Who opposeth and exalteth himself above all that is called God, or that is worshipped; so that he as God sitteth in the temple of God, shewing himself that he is God."*

Notice again that the definite article "the" indicates there is only one "son of perdition." Inasmuch as the title is given to one man who lived in the past in a state of perdition, and to a man to arise in the future who will be in a state of perdition when he comes, we have to consider the possibility that both men, Judas and the Antichrist, are one and the same person.

The words of Jesus concerning Judas in John 6:70 are also of particular interest: *". . . Have not I chosen you twelve, and one of you is a devil?"* The most quoted Bible authorities on the Greek text agree that the indefinite article "a" in the verse was added by the translators. What Jesus actually said of Judas was, *". . . one of you* [meaning Judas] *is devil. . . ."* *Fausset's Bible Encyclopedia and Dictionary* says of this scripture that the Greek word for devil used by Jesus, in referring to Judas, does not

> *". . . merely mean demon, the Greek word always used for the evil spirit possessing a body, but 'devil,' used only of Satan himself."*

In the selecting of another to take the place of Judas, Luke wrote in Acts 1:25:

". . . of this ministry and apostleship, from which Judas by transgression fell, that he might go to his own place."

Again, we should ponder the meaning of Judas going to "his own place," a reference applied to no other human being at death.

In the Old Testament, Israel is warned against the wicked and deceitful prince who will intercede to make a covenant for them, but then after three and a half years, he commits the Abomination of Desolation prophesied by Daniel. According to the Bible, this evil deed consists of stopping the daily sacrifice in the Temple, informing all the world that the biblical account of Jesus Christ and His claim to be the Messiah is a myth, and he then presents his claim to be Christ. With the aid of the False Prophet, the Antichrist will demand that all the world worship him as God or be killed. It will be at this time that the False Messiah turns against the Jews, and then they will have to flee to the wilderness and the mountains to hide. Most prophetic Bible scholars believe Israel's hiding place to be in Petra (Matt. 24:15-21; Rev. 12). The reason for Israel's flight is presented in type in Psalm 55:11-14:

"Wickedness is in the midst thereof: deceit and guile depart not from her streets. For it was not an enemy that reproached me; then I could have borne it: neither was it he that hated me that did magnify himself against me; then I would have hid myself from him: But it was thou, a man mine equal, my guide, and mine acquaintance."

Dr. Arthur W. Pink, noted Bible expositor, said of this messianic psalm:

"These verses describe not only the base treachery of Judas toward Christ, but they also announce how he shall yet, when reincarnated in the Antichrist, betray and desert Israel. The relation of Antichrist to Israel will be precisely the same as that of Judas to Christ. He will pose as the friend of the Jews, but later he will come out in his true character. In the Tribulation period, the nation shall taste the bitterness of betrayal and desertion by one who masqueraded as a 'familiar friend.' Hence, we have here the first hint that the Antichrist will be Judas reincarnated."

More knowledge was given to the Apostle John by the Holy Spirit about the person and reign of Antichrist than any other writer of Holy Scripture. Only John described this agent of Satan as Antichrist, the total negative of the Lord Jesus Christ. By reading in sequence the Gospel of John, the First Epistle of John, and the Revelation of John, we have a composite picture of the beginning and the end of the "son of perdition."

Judas was the only one of the twelve disciples who was not a Galilean, and little is known about his family or background. There is not a good word said about him in the entire Bible. Psalm 109 provides a remarkable prophetic view of the relationship of Judas to Jesus. Verses six through eleven speak of Judas thusly:

"Set thou a wicked man over him: and let Satan stand at his right hand. When he shall be judged, let him be condemned: and let his prayer

become sin. Let his days be few; and let another take his office. . . . Let the extortioner catch all that he hath; and let the strangers spoil his labor."

This part of the messianic Psalm 109 refers to the betrayal of Jesus by Judas, his evil nature, the buying of a potter's field with the bribe money, and the appointment of Matthias to take the place of the fallen disciple. Verses thirteen through fifteen of the same psalm relate to the judgment Judas brought upon himself for his terrible sin:

"Let his posterity be cut off; and in the generation following let their name be blotted out. Let the iniquity of his fathers be remembered with the Lord; and let not the sin of his mother be blotted out. Let them be before the Lord continually, that he may cut off the memory of them from the earth."

Judas was a tool of the religious element of the generation in Israel at the time Jesus Christ offered them the Kingdom. In the Temple Discourse (Matt. 23), Jesus pronounced judgment on that generation. Jesus was born in 4 B.C., so the Temple Discourse was delivered in A.D. 30. Forty is the Jewish number of testing. The generation of Israel who refused to believe God and cross the Jordan wandered in the wilderness for forty years, and they were cut off. At the end of forty years, after Jesus pronounced judgment upon the generation who refused to believe that He was the Messiah, that generation was also cut off. But Jesus spoke of a second generation in the Olivet Discourse. He said of the signs given in Matthew 24 concerning His second coming, *". . . This generation shall not pass, till all these things be fulfilled"* (v. 34). In the Temple Discourse, Jesus warned of another judgment that would come on a second generation—the generation of Israel in the days of His return. The second generation of Israelites spoken about in the Olivet Discourse will see the refounding of Israel as a nation. They will be the ones who will receive the false messiah who will come in his own name (John 5:43). Two-thirds of the second generation will be cut off from the kingdom (Zech. 13:8-9). The remaining one-third of the last generation will say, *"Blessed is he that cometh in the name of the Lord"* (Matt. 23:39).

The prophecies concerning Judas in Psalm 109 relating to his treachery are divided into two different generations. God keeps time by the Jew, but when the Jew is out of the land, time stops. Thus, the first twelve verses relate to Judas in his betrayal of Jesus at the advent of Christ. The remainder of the psalm concerning the judgment of Judas when he will be completely and forever cut off, and his name remembered no more, is connected with the second advent of the Lord. The things which are to happen to Judas in the second generation seem to parallel the final end of Antichrist.

There are some who believe that the Antichrist will be a great world personality who will be killed, brought back to life, and possessed by the Devil. However, there are sound scriptural reasons for believing that the Antichrist will be an evil man who has lived in the past, and Satan is keeping him in perdition, waiting for world conditions to develop favorably where he can be brought forth. The Scriptures indicate this is to be the case, and Judas Iscariot, **"the** son of perdition" is the most likely candidate.

Some believe that the Antichrist will be Nero come back from the dead, and many good Bible scholars believe he will be a great political personality who will be assassinated and then brought back to life during the Tribulation. We have presented our reasons for believing that Judas was at least a type of the Antichrist, or possibly the Beast himself.

Isaiah prophesied about the Antichrist:

"Hell from beneath is moved for thee to meet thee at thy coming: it stirreth up the dead for thee, even all the chief ones of the earth; it hath raised up from their thrones all the kings of the nations. . . . Thou shalt not be joined with them in burial, because thou hast destroyed thy land, and slain thy people . . ." (Isa. 14:9,20).

Isaiah's prophecy about Antichrist corresponds with Revelation 19:19-21:

"And I saw the beast, and the kings of the earth, and their armies, gathered together to make war against him that sat on the horse, and against his army. And the beast was taken, and with him the false prophet that wrought miracles before him, with which he deceived them that had received the mark of the beast, and them that worshipped his image. These both were cast alive into a lake of fire burning with brimstone. And the remnant were slain with the sword of him that sat upon the horse, which sword proceeded out of his mouth: and all the fowls were filled with their flesh."

As prophesied by Isaiah, the grave of the Antichrist will not be made with the slain of his armies. Hell is already waiting for him; his eternal fate has already been pre-ordained by God. Both the Antichrist and the False Prophet will be cast **alive** into the lake of fire. As Isaiah 14:11 indicates, their bodies will endure eternal torment.

Chapter Twelve

Death and Resurrection In the Millennium

Verses one through nine of Revelation 20 provide a brief overview of the Millennium, Kingdom age, or thousand-year reign of Jesus Christ on the earth. Satan has operated as the prince of the world, and successfully brought a rebellion against God in all nations. The first events of the Millennium include the binding of Satan and then casting him into the bottomless pit for one thousand years. Just what this entails is only understandable within the spiritual realm of God. The nearest thing to Hell to our understanding would be a bottomless pit, what astronomers would classify as a black hole. In Revelation 12, John sees Satan being cast down to the earth, and in Revelation 20, the Devil is bound and confined where he will not be able to deceive the nations and tempt mankind for one thousand years. Then, we read that after the one thousand years, Satan must be turned loose once more for a little season. Why must Satan be loosed? Many Bible scholars contend that the Devil must be let loose again to see if after one thousand years of peace, plenty, and righteousness, man will be able to just say "No" to the Devil.

In Revelation 20:4, the following events are foretold:

1. The establishing of thrones, meaning political positions in the government of Jesus Christ. The twelve apostles were promised a throne, ruling over the twelve tribes of Israel. This promise will be fulfilled during the Millennium.

2. The delegation of governmental authority, or judgment. The Chief Judge of all nations during the Millennium will be Jesus Christ. We read in two scriptures in Revelation that Jesus Christ will rule all nations with a rod of iron (Rev. 12:5; Rev. 19:12). In Revelation 2:27, it is promised that overcomers will likewise rule the nations with a rod of iron, even as Jesus received this authority from God the Father. The overcomers apparently will be those during the Tribulation who were beheaded for claiming the blood of Jesus Christ for salvation and refusing to take the mark of the Beast or worship the Antichrist as God. These will likewise rule with Jesus for the entire one thousand years. Beheading was a method of execution adopted by the ancients because it was terminal, and it was believed that beheading would separate soul and body forever, and there would be no resurrection. Revelation 20:4 proves this heathenish belief to be an error. Rome used two methods of execution: crucifixion for non-Romans, and beheading for Roman citizens. Jesus was crucified, but Paul, being a Roman citizen, was beheaded. Beheading remained the customary method of execution for nations which broke off the Roman Empire. The *Encyclopaedia Britannica* gives the records of crude machines with a weighted blade which dropped down upon the necks of prisoners severing heads from bodies. One of the oldest

machines was called the "maiden" in Scotland. King Edward VIII liked to behead his wives to get rid of them. Beheading was used as a method of capital punishment in Germany, Italy, and other European countries. On December 1, 1789, Dr. Guillotine, a member of the French Assembly, sponsored legislation that

". . . in all cases of capital punishment it shall be same kind—that is, decapitation—and it shall be executed by means of a machine."

This is how the beheading machine became known as the guillotine. Inasmuch as the empire of the Antichrist will be the Revived Roman Empire, it follows that beheading will be the method of execution. However, those who will be beheaded during the Tribulation will be raised in an immortal body and reign with Jesus Christ.

3. The resurrection of Old Testament saints: The resurrection of the Old Testament is associated with the coming of a Redeemer. Job declared:

"For I know that my redeemer liveth, and that he shall stand at the latter day upon the earth: And though after my skin worms destroy this body, yet in my flesh shall I see God: Whom I shall see for myself, and mine eyes shall behold, and not another . . ." (Job 19:25-27).

Daniel placed the time of Israel's resurrection when *". . . there shall be a time of trouble, such as never was since there was a nation."* Then the prophet said:

". . . many of them that sleep in the dust of the earth shall awake, some to everlasting life, and some to shame and everlasting contempt" (Dan. 12:1-2).

The resurrection of Israel is also placed at the last days when the Messiah would come in Isaiah 26 and Ezekiel 37. The lot of the Old Testament saints in resurrection is earthly. The lot of the church in resurrection is heavenly places or worlds in outer space. It has been suggested that when the number of the church reaches the number of angels who followed Satan and left their heavenly places, then the Rapture will occur. It is difficult to find a Millennial, earthly promise to the church; however, Revelation 20:6 seems to include the church:

"Blessed and holy is he that hath part in the first resurrection: on such the second death hath no power, but they shall be priests of God and of Christ, and shall reign with him a thousand years."

It is evident beyond dispute that the first resurrection includes first, Jesus Christ, then the church of the dispensation of grace, then the saved of the Tribulation period, then the Old Testament saints, and in that order. All the others who have lived and died since Adam will not be raised until the end of the Millennium. These are the lost dead. We read in Revelation 20:5, *"But the rest of the dead lived not again until the thousand years were finished. . . ."*

Judgment Of the Nations

We read the introduction to the prophetic discourse on the coming judgment of the nations in Matthew 25:31-33:

"When the Son of man shall come in his glory, and all the holy angels with him, then shall he sit upon the throne of his glory: And before him shall be gathered all nations: and he shall separate them one from another, as a shepherd divideth his sheep from the goats: And he shall see the sheep on his right hand, but the goats on the left."

All commentaries by scholars I have ever read put this event immediately after the Battle of Armageddon. I think this interpretation is bad chronology. We read that when Jesus Christ returns He will sit, or rule, upon the throne of His glory. This will be the throne of David which the angels said He would sit upon at His birth. He will rule all nations with a rod of iron. The rules will be that the kings of nations come up to Jerusalem to worship Him. If there is disobedience, or if Egypt does not come up, upon those nations will no rain fall until they learn obedience. If any curse the Jews rather than bless them, these nations will be accursed. The rules for national obedience in the Millennium will be the beatitudes of Matthew 5. Those nations which are now accounted righteous under the thousand-year reign of Jesus Christ will go into the New Heaven and the New Earth and, as we read in Matthew 25:46, "life eternal." The goat nations will appear at the Great White Throne Judgment.

Nature Of the Millennium

As Joel, Isaiah, and other prophets foretold, in the Millennium there will be no weapons of war, no national or international conflicts. Satan will be bound so as not to tempt men or nations with greed and lust. However, this does not mean that man will not sin. The excuse, "the Devil made me do it," is a poor one. We are told in Isaiah 65:20 that during the Kingdom age, a sinner being a hundred years old will be accursed. In other words, during the Millennium, a sinner will be given one hundred years to repent and obey the Lord. The law will be enforced from Jerusalem, and sinners who continually violate the law will be cut off. Other than the death of the ungodly or sinners, there will be no death during the Millennium. As it was before the flood, those in the Millennium will live to be almost one thousand years old. We are told that God's people will live to be as old as trees.

Environmental problems will be solved during the Millennium, deserts will become productive farmland, and there will be peace in the animal world—the lamb will lie down with the wolves. The curse on nature came because of sin. Adam sinned and nature was cursed. In Noah's day, mankind became exceedingly sinful and nature was cursed again. In these days, there is much concern, and nations hold summit meetings regarding the ecology. The problem is as the Bible declares: the more sinful the human race becomes, the sicker the environment becomes. Paul wrote in Romans 8:18-23 that the whole creation, including the birds and animals, are waiting for the completion of the first resurrection when the weight of sin from the ground will be lifted.

No man has yet lived to be a thousand years. One day is as a thousand years with God, and the Lord told Adam the day he sinned he would die. The account by John regarding the termination of the thousand-year reign of Jesus Christ encompasses the release of Satan from the bottomless pit for a little season. The Tribulation is referred to in Revelation 6:11 as a little season, so Satan is allowed only a few years at most to do his dirty work. Even after a thousand years of peace, plenty, and perfect government, man fails again for the seventh time. As the armies of the nations come to destroy Jerusalem and the camp of the saints, fire comes down from Heaven and destroys them all. Whether all the people on earth, not including the resurrected saints, are destroyed is not clear. From the account of the judgments of the nations in Matthew 25, it appears that only the goat nations will be annihilated, because the sheep nations are promised eternal life.

During the Millennium, according to Ezekiel 40-48, the tribes of Israel will again be divided and inhabit the land given them by God. There will be a huge Millennial Temple, which according to Zechariah 6, Jesus Christ Himself will build. The waters of the Dead Sea will become alive with fish from the Mediterranean Sea. According to Isaiah 35 and 65, anyone at the age of one hundred will be considered to be a youth and all illnesses, disease, and physical disabilities will be healed. But the lie of Satan is that God is just not giving man everything that he deserves, so when Satan is set free for a few months to test once more the free will of men, the human race makes the wrong choice once more.

Some Bible scholars link Gog and Magog of Revelation 20:8 with the same conspiracy in Ezekiel 38 and 39, but it cannot be the same event. After the battle of Ezekiel 38, Israel spends seven years cleaning the land. After the battle of Revelation 20:8, the earth is burned up. After the battle of Ezekiel 38, a remnant of the invading army is left. After the battle of Revelation 20:8, none are left. Gog and Magog have a limited number of allies in the battle of Ezekiel 38; in the battle of Revelation 20:8, Gog and Magog are joined by all nations. The center of Satan's rebellion is located in the race of Gog and Magog, and this seems to be the reason for the greatest anti-God conspiracy the world has ever experienced within the Soviet Union of this century.

Will man ever be satisfied with his own estate in life? Not in this present earth and social order. Nevertheless, beyond the Millennium lies another chance for mankind to live at peace with himself and with God.

Chapter Thirteen

The Great White Throne Judgment

---

*"And I saw a great white throne, and him
that sat on it, from whose face the earth and the
heaven fled away; and there was found no place
for them"* (Rev. 20:11).

With the final rebellion of mankind against God at
the end of the Millennium, the earth and the heaven
(meaning the first heaven, the atmosphere) disappeared.
This event will not be simply a renovation of this present
earth. The scripture states without qualification that this
earth will have served its purpose; it will not be in
evidence. War against God, which is sin against God,
contaminates. Rather than curse creation again, God
makes a new planet, like the world was when Adam and
Eve were first created.

Of God's everlasting covenant with Israel, Isaiah
prophesied:

*"For as the new heavens and the new earth,
which I will make, shall remain before me, saith
the Lord, so shall your seed and your name
remain"* (Isa. 66:22).

The Apostle Peter wrote of the destruction of this earth:

> *"But the day of the Lord will come as a thief in the night; in the which* [in the thousand years] *the heavens shall pass away with a great noise, and the elements shall melt with fervent heat, the earth also and the works that are therein shall be burned up. . . . Nevertheless we* [the saved], *according to his promise, look for new heavens and a new earth, wherein dwelleth righteousness"* (2 Pet. 3:10,13).

How will this happen? We have to remember that Paul said the things which appear are made out of things which do not appear (Heb. 11:3). Scientists now say that everything in the universe came into being in an instant—from something, possibly no bigger than a basketball, in an instant. But the Bible says that all matter appeared as God spoke. The two positions are now very close to being one—God spoke. God can also speak and everything will disappear. Atoms are seen only by their activity. If the shells were stripped from atoms, a million people could dance on the head of a pin.

A great white throne is set, called to order, and the earth and the heavens fly away—disappear. Why? Because only that which is righteous can stand before this mighty, holy throne. Certainly, this earth is not clean from sin, and the heavens which have been defiled by the ungodly activity of Satan are not clean (Job 15:15).

> *"And I saw the dead, small and great, stand before God; and the books were opened: and another book was opened, which is the book of*

life: and the dead were judged out of those things which were written in the books, according to their works" (Rev. 20:12).

All who were not raised in the first resurrection will be raised in the second resurrection to stand at the Great White Throne Judgment. I do not believe that anyone saved during the Millennium will stand at this judgment. Only sinners who have died during the thousand years will be raised to appear at this judgment. All the saved—the righteous of the Millennium—will be taken over this judgment into the New Heavens and the New Earth. So all those resurrected to stand judgment at the Great White Throne will be the lost dead from Cain to the last rebellion.   Christians will stand before the Judgment Seat (Bema) of Jesus Christ to receive a reward for their works, deeds, or service (1 Cor. 3; 2 Cor. 5:10). But nothing is said about any believer appearing before the Judgment Seat of Christ being cast into Hell or the lake of fire. The opposite is true; though a Christian receive no reward, or lose his reward, he will be saved. That is the plain truth of scripture. On the other hand, nothing is said about any appearing before the Great White Throne Judgment being saved—all are condemned.

The identity of the Great Judge at the White Throne is, of course, Jesus Christ as Daniel and John saw Him: awesome, powerful, omnipotent, holy. Only such a judge would be worthy to send a man to an eternal Hell. We read in John 5:22 that God the Father judges no man, but He has committed all judgment to His Son.

Jesus said that if He was lifted up that He would draw all men unto Him. Daniel described the Great White Throne Judgment scene in these words:

"I beheld till the thrones were cast down, and the Ancient of days did sit, whose garment was white as snow, and the hair of his head like the pure wool: his throne was like the fiery flame, and his wheels as burning fire. A fiery stream issued and came forth from before him: thousand thousands ministered unto him, and ten thousand times ten thousand stood before him: the judgment was set, and the books were opened" (Dan. 7:9-10).

We are informed in verse fifteen of Revelation 20 that the resurrected dead standing at the Great White Throne will be cast into the lake of fire because their names are not written in the Book of Life. So we must examine this Book of Life with the light of Scripture.

1. Some theologians believe that at conception, the name, or identity, of every person is written in the Book of Life. David wrote in Psalm 139:16 that in God's book, all his body members were written. Then, if that person dies without accepting God's way of salvation, his name is blotted out of the Book of Life. Moses pleaded with God in Exodus 32:31-33:

   "And Moses returned unto the Lord, and said, Oh, this people have sinned a great sin, and have made them gods of gold. Yet now, if thou wilt forgive their sin—; and if not, blot me, I pray thee, out of thy book which thou hast written. And the Lord said unto Moses, Whosoever hath sinned against me, him will I blot out of my book."

We know from Romans 3:23, ". . . *all have sinned, and come short of the glory of God.* "From the Old Testament position, it would appear that all who die in their sins will be blotted out of the Book of Life.

2. From the New Testament doctrinal position of the church, the security of the believer, it appears that the Christian's name is irreversibly written in the Book of Life:

   "And I intreat thee also, true yokefellow, help those women which laboured with me in the gospel, with Clement also, and with other my fellowlabourers, whose names are in the book of life" (Phil. 4:3).

   "He that overcometh . . . I will not blot out his name out of the book of life . . ." (Rev. 3:5).

   According to the Gospel, Christians have overcome the world through faith in Jesus Christ.

3. In the book of Revelation, we read of those whose names are not written in the Book of Life:

   "And all that dwell upon the earth shall worship him, whose names are not written in the book of life of the Lamb slain from the foundation of the world" (Rev. 13:8).

   ". . . and they that dwell on the earth shall wonder, whose names were not written in the book of life from the foundation of the world, when they behold the beast that was, and is not, and yet is" (Rev. 17:8).

It is also made clear from Revelation 21:27 that only those whose names are written in the Lamb's Book of Life will be allowed to inhabit the New Heavens or the New Earth. All others, the resurrected lost dead, will be suffering eternal agony in the lake of fire.

To reconcile the overall biblical teachings about the Book of Life is most difficult. There are some truths about the mysteries of God that will not be fully understood until Christians are given the answers in Heaven. As far as those mentioned in Revelation whose names were never written in the Book of Life, these are referred to as those who will worship the Antichrist as the true christ. When the Lamb was slain for sin from the foundation of the world, these names were not even entered in His book. The foreknowledge of God is absolute, because He lives in eternity. Just as Christians are preordained from the foundation of the world to live eternally with Jesus Christ (Rom. 8:29-30), it appears that those who take the mark of the Beast have been preordained to spend eternity with him in the lake of fire. This does not mean they are not included in "whosoever will," but it does mean these people will consciously, and of their own choice, worship Antichrist instead of Jesus Christ, and God knew from the foundation of the world that they would make this decision.

At the Great White Throne Judgment, there will be two sets of books. It could be that in the first set, the name of every person conceived is written, and the Great Judge checks the name in the first book and then checks to see if the name appears in the second book, the Book of Life. It is also possible that the first set of books contains a record of every sin committed by those standing before this final bar of judgment, because we read *"the dead were judged out of those things written in the books, according to their works.*" How many sins does the average person commit in the average life span? A thousand, a million, a billion? How long will the lost suffer in the lake of fire for each sin committed? A thousand years, a million years, a billion years? All we know is that the torment will be eternal. And, will there be degrees of punishment in the lake of fire, just as there will be degrees of rewards in Heaven? The wording of Revelation 20:11-15 does seem to indicate such to be true.

Jesus said in Matthew 25:41 that Hell was prepared for the Devil and his angels, and in other scriptures it is revealed that Hell was enlarged to receive men and women who would die in their sins. Hell is a confining place of torment until the Great White Throne Judgment. In Revelation 20:13, we read that at the last judgment, Hell will deliver up the souls of the dead, and then, both death and Hell will be cast into the lake of fire.

Paul wrote in 1 Corinthians 15:24-26:

"Then cometh the end, when he shall have delivered up the kingdom to God, even the Father, when he shall have put down all rule and all authority and power. For he must reign, till he hath put all enemies under his feet. The last enemy that shall be destroyed is death."

There is a saying that death kills more people than anything else. But at the end of the Millennium at the Great White Throne Judgment, death will be destroyed by Jesus Christ. No person will ever have to worry about, or face, death anymore. The last enemy will be destroyed. In these days of high-pressure multimedia politics, the candidate promises everything possible—better housing, better schools, better jobs, better environment, better health, and even longer life. But one thing they cannot promise—no death. Jesus Christ is the only One in the universe Who can promise you that.

Beyond the Great White Throne Judgment lies an eternal, never-ending lake of fire. Is such a thing scientifically possible? Scientists now tell us that in the process of the Law of Entropy, stars nova, meaning that they exhaust the supply of hydrogen and the fusion atomic process goes out of control. The star (and our sun is a medium-sized star) gets hot and bright for seven to fourteen days, the atoms are stripped of their shells, and the entire mass is compressed into a small area where the gravity is so intense no light can escape. Isaiah, John, Jesus, and Joel described such an event for our sun. Astronomers call novas black holes. They are black, the hottest place in the universe, bottomless, and the semi-solid atomic pile could be classified as a lake. If our sun were to nova, all nine planets of our solar system, including the earth, would be sucked into its vortex. Whether such a black hole will be the lake of fire may be questionable; nevertheless, there will be an eternal lake of fire where the Devil, the fallen angels, and all who die in their sins will be forever separated from God in eternal torment.

The only way to escape is to have their names written in the Lamb's Book of Life with the blood of Jesus Christ than can never be blotted out.

Chapter Fourteen

New Heaven and New Earth

The scene following the Great White Throne Judgment opens up a New Heaven and New Earth. We are not told if the New Earth will be larger than the present earth, or even if it will be in the present solar system. There is a mention of no need for the sun and the moon, and this could mean they are no more, or it could mean their light is simply not needed.

The first thing that John sees in the New Heaven and the New Earth is the New Jerusalem coming down through the heavens to land on the earth. As a description of the New Jerusalem is given in detail in Revelation 21 and 22, we will not take time and space to enlarge upon the picture which the apostle painted in beautiful and glowing terminology. Suffice it to say the New Jerusalem will be fifteen hundred square miles, about the same size as that part of the United States west of the Mississippi River. This is the city that we are told in Hebrews 11:10 that Abraham looked for. This is the city which the Golden City of Israel, Jerusalem, typifies. Some believe the New Jerusalem will be a perfect fifteen hundred mile cube; others believe it will be in the shape of a pyramid. Regardless, it will be a tremendously large city. We also read of it in Hebrews 12:22-24:

"But ye are come unto mount Sion, and unto the city of the living God, the heavenly Jerusalem, and to an innumerable company of angels, To the general assembly and church of the firstborn, which are written in heaven, and to God the Judge of all, and to the spirits of just men made perfect, And to Jesus the mediator of the new covenant, and to the blood of sprinkling, that speaketh better things than that of Abel."

Who will inhabit the New Jerusalem? God the Father, Jesus Christ, and a host of angels, too many to count. We are told that the general assembly and church of the firstborn will be in the New Jerusalem. This must be the church of the dispensation of grace, the completed body of Christians which God has called out of the Gentile nations. Also, the spirits of just men made perfect will be in the New Jerusalem, and these surely are the Old Testament saints. Everyone from Abel to the Tribulation saints who have been included in the first resurrection will be in the New Jerusalem. This does not mean the members of the church will be confined to the New Jerusalem, because from the second chapter of Ephesians it seems evident that Christians will also be involved in ruling over heavenly places throughout the universe.

On the New Earth, John sees nations. God determined seventy nations from the grandsons of Noah, and it would seem that this will be the number of nations in the New Earth. Where do the citizens of these nations come from? They are ones who remained faithful to the King of kings during the Millennium. In the beginning, God, Who is love, created a man and a woman to multiply and inhabit the earth. This man and woman were given a free will. They could obey and love God their Creator, or they had the option of refusing to love and serve Him. God could have created Adam and Eve without a free will, but they would not have been capable of true love. During the Millennium, Jesus Christ, the Creator of all things, will reign and rule for a thousand years. Jesus said to the disciples, *"If you love me, keep my commandments."* During the Millennium, people n earth will prove their love by worshipping and keeping the commandments of Jesus Christ. At the end of the Millennium, Satan will again deceive many nations, but those who love the Lord their God with all their hearts will remain faithful. Thus, God will have accomplished His purpose—to have an earth inhabited with men and women who love Him out of their own free will and choice.

We notice in Revelation 21:2-8 that in the New Earth and the New Jerusalem, there will be no sorrow, no tears, no pain, no death, no crime, no law breakers, no sinners. All the deaths, tears, crime, and sin committed on this earth is due to Adam and Eve disobeying one little commandment of God. In the New Earth, there will be no sin or sinners, no rebellion, no disobedience to God's will. Sin will be gone forever.

The New Earth is Paradise, or Eden, restored. The very same environment, the very same Tree of Life. Adam and Eve could have eaten of the Tree of Life and lived forever. The citizens of the nations in the New Earth will have continual access to the Tree of Life. They will walk in the light of the New Jerusalem and travel in and out of the city.

Now the question may be asked: How can we know whether or not at some point in time or eternity, the men and women of the nations that inhabit the New Earth will not choose to again disobey God as Adam and Eve did? There are two things which were in the Garden of Eden that will be missing in the New Earth. These two things are Satan and the Tree of Knowledge of Good and Evil.

The things that politicians and social planners tell us we need today are:

1. Better law enforcement—yet, the more politicians and jails we have, the more criminals there are.
2. Better housing—yet, the housing projects of the Sixties have become the slums and centers of social conflict in the Nineties.
3. Better education—yet, the more schools and teachers in the educational system, the more social, economic, criminal, and racial problems there are.
4. Better government—yet, the more governmental institutions are established and the more money given government to operate, the less effective it becomes.
5. Better national health programs—yet, in spite of additional billions in health care, heart disease, cancer, and plagues like AIDS are on the increase.
6. Better food distribution—yet, even though there are surpluses and the affluent eat better than ever in history, hunger, famine, and starvation stalks the earth.
7. Better jobs and higher pay—yet, as the majority has money to buy better houses and bigger cars, more is spent on pleasure and lust as in the days of Noah.

In the Millennium, mankind will have better law enforcement, better housing, better education, better government, better health care, bigger food supplies, and better jobs—not only for a few years, but for one thousand years. God will give the nations all these things to prove His justice; that man's salvation and future is not to be found in himself, but in the God Who made him.

I have been to the Ziggurat of Ur. Nearby is the architecturally perfect tomb of an ancient queen who ruled from 2050 B.C., or before. She was buried with her chariots, servants, and jewels in the expectation of a future life. In ancient Egypt, the dead were buried in a fetal position, expecting a resurrection. The pyramids of Egypt were built by the pharaohs as gateways to the heavens in the life beyond. I have been to the Ming Tombs and the Ching Tombs in China, ornate and extensive tombs for the emperors and empresses of these dynasties. I have been to Karnak, the most extensive network of tombs in the world, then crossed over the Nile River to the unbelievable architectural wonder of the tomb of Hatshepsut, built by her lover. Around the mountain lies the Valley of the Kings, tombs of other Egyptian royalty where their mummies were laid to await the afterlife. I have seen the bodies of Lenin and Mao Tse Tung, lying in vacuum glass coffins; Flanders Field where the fallen of World War One were buried; and Arlington Cemetery, dotted with hundreds of thousands of crosses, and witnessed the amazing changing of the guard. I have been to Ephesus, Pergamos, Patmos, Petra, and dozens of other places familiar in ancient history and viewed the thousands of sumptuous and decorative tombs prepared especially for the dead. I have stood upon the Mount of Olives and beheld the tombs of the prophets and the thousands of tombs and graves that cover the western slope, down through the Garden of Gethsemane, through the Kidron Valley, right up to the Golden Gate. Those in centuries past have buried their dead on Mount Olivet, because the Bible promises that the Messiah will one day stand upon this mountain and the dead will be brought up out of these graves and tombs in a resurrected body.

All these tombs and graves testify to the undeniable fact that as far back as the history of the human race can be traced, man has always believed that there was a life, a future, beyond death. There has been something in the nature, instinct, and mind of men and women that there is a resurrection.

The Christian's faith in resurrection lies in the resurrection of Jesus Christ:

> *"But now is Christ risen from the dead, and become the firstfruits of them that slept. For since by man came death, by man came also the resurrection of the dead. For as in Adam all die, even so in Christ shall all be made alive"* (1 Cor. 15:20-22).

In our preaching, in our books, in our testimony, unless we get Jesus Christ up out of the grave, we are indeed of all men most miserable. Our message is always: Because Jesus Christ lives, we shall live also.

All creation, including the angels of Heaven, await the resurrection and Rapture of the church. Signs in the heavens and in the earth indicate this glorious event is near. If Jesus Christ should call today for those who belong to Him to rise up and join Him in the air, be changed in a moment into an immortal, glorified body, would you be ready?

> *"For if we believe that Jesus died and rose again, even so them also which sleep in Jesus will God bring with him.*
>
> *"For this we say unto you by the word of*

the Lord, that we which are alive and remain unto the coming of the Lord shall not prevent them which are asleep.

"For the Lord himself shall descend from heaven with a shout, with the voice of the archangel, and with the trump of God: and the dead in Christ shall rise first:

"Then we which are alive and remain shall be caught up together with them in the clouds, to meet the Lord in the air: and so shall we ever be with the Lord.

"Wherefore comfort one another with these words" (1 Thess. 4:13-18).

In view of the glories awaiting we who have been born again through faith in Jesus Christ, we pray the last prayer recorded in the Bible, *"Even so, come, Lord Jesus."*